Maine Island Kids

Sweaters and Stories from Offshore

North Island Designs

Maine Island Kids
Sweaters and Stories from Offshore

by Chellie Pingree and Debby Anderson
Photos by Peter Ralston

20 KNITTING PATTERNS FROM
NORTH ISLAND DESIGNS

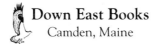
Down East Books
Camden, Maine

ISBN 0-89272-316-5

Photography by Peter Ralston
Design and production by Michael Mahan Graphics
Editing by Helen Popp
Typeset by Black Spruce Type/Graphics

Printed and bound in Hong Kong through Four Colour Imports

10   9   8   7   6   5   4   3

Down East Books, Camden, Maine

Table of Contents

Maine Island Kids

This is our second knitting book. After surviving the first one, we decided to go on with a second, a book devoted to patterns for children. Along with providing you with the designs that we have created over the past few years, we have made some additions that we hope will enrich the book for you. We produce these books for more than one reason and hope that they are more than "just knitting books."

Obviously, we love to see people knitting, although from our first book you may remember that we admitted that only Debby is proficient at the craft. We encourage you to knit not only for the end product, which will be lovely and a joy for you to wear or share with someone, but for the experience as well. Debby loves to knit because it is "good for her soul." It provides a time when you can clear your head, focus your thoughts and concentrate on your project— even in a crowded room or an unpleasant place. It is a chance to create your own island—yourself and the project, a feeling of total absorption, with an end product.

We decided to continue with our stories in this book since many of you let us know it enhanced your enjoyment of the patterns. We also added some writing from the kids in our community because we felt that they could reflect, in a very personal way, the experience of being a kid on an island. We gathered these stories by speaking with their teachers at school and sponsoring a "contest" of sorts. The idea of a contest was difficult because we knew that what every student had to say would be unique and special and would reflect what each felt, so we didn't want there to be "winners and losers." We knew, however, that we would need to be able to choose those pieces which worked into our theme. We decided to give every student who entered a gift certificate, making each of them a winner.

As we suspected, each piece was wonderful. We have had to choose those that fit our space limitations, but we were pleased with all that the students contributed and felt that it was a privilege to be able to include some of it.

We have also included some of the people who make up our community in our photographs . Although this is a small selection, we felt that it may contribute to your image of our business and life on an island and the sense of community we appreciate and encourage you to seek in your own lives.

Before You Begin Knitting These Patterns...

For those of you who are knitting with our patterns for the first time we've repeated the advice from our first book.

Gauge

Before you start any project—*check your gauge.* All sweaters are designed to be knit with a certain number of stitches to the inch and this is far more important than the suggested needle size. The most important step is to choose the size of needles that will allow you to achieve the required number of stitches to the inch.

To do this, knit a small swatch about 20 stitches wide by three inches high using the main color and the larger of the suggested needles. When you are done, gently press with a damp cloth, then let it cool. Now, measure two inches across and count the stitches; divide this number by two and you've got your gauge. If you have fewer stitches per inch than the gauge given in the pattern, decrease the size of your needles; if too many, increase the size of your needles, and knit a swatch again. This step is very important to achieve the garment you want, no matter how many years you have been knitting.

Ribbing

When you are casting on the lower edge, remember that the ribbing is intended to be elastic as the garment is worn. If you have a tendency to cast on too tightly, use a larger needle to cast on the stitches. Also remember to bind off neck stitches loosely so that the ribbing can stretch to go over the head.

When a pattern calls for K1, P1 ribbing it is hard to go wrong. However, you will notice that in some of my patterns I have used a K2, P1 ribbing. When my sister-in-law was just learning to knit, she very ambitiously started the chicken sweater. The next time she came to visit she proudly showed me the front and I noticed she had done exactly what I said—K2, P1, but on both sides! It produced a very unique look, to say the least, but it will not have the stretch of ribbing done the correct way. To avoid having her start over I suggested she duplicate it on the back and cuffs. The lesson here is—work your ribbing K2, P1 on the right side and K1, P2 when you turn the piece over.

Multi-Color Knitting

Knitting with two or more colors is very easy and if you have never done it before, now is a perfect time to start!! Knit a small swatch to practice and you will be surprised how simple it is.

When knitting with two colors, don't tie a new color on until you have knit a few stitches with it—then go back and make a simple small knot. If you can weave the end in without making a knot at all, it is better, but often if you don't attach it somehow, the stitches will have a tendency to loosen up. When you are carrying colors, it is important to carry the unused color for no more than three or four stitches before twisting the yarns together. If you carry it further without twisting you will end up with a long piece on the inside that can easily be caught when putting on the sweater.

It is good to use bobbins and short pieces of yarn and even attach new balls of the background color rather than carry the colors behind. This way the design will lay flat and not pucker. You are left with ends to weave in but try to relax and enjoy it—a nice sweater takes time to complete.

Mistakes in two color knitting can be corrected by duplicate stitch after the garment is complete. Duplicate stitch is also good in areas where only a small amount of color is called for. A color out of place here or there won't make a great difference. As my mother used to say, "It will never be noticed on a galloping horse!"

Putting Your Sweater Together

When all of the pieces have been finished, it is very important to press (block) them before sewing them together. To sew the seams, put the right sides together, take a straight needle (about a number 5) and use it as a large pin to hold the pieces while sewing them together using a back stitch. Sew the shoulders first (unless the pattern has called for knitting them together), then the neck ribbing, the side seams and sleeve seams. Last of all turn the body wrong side out and insert the sleeve, right sides together and match the seams at the underarms and shoulders. After the sleeve cap is fitted, sew it using a back stitch and press all of your seams.

Choosing a size

Figuring out what size to make is a very logical process. Begin by finding a sweater that fits the way you (or your sweater recipient) really like a sweater to fit. Then, measure across the chest, the sleeve length, the length of the sweater, etc. Here is where the stitch gauge becomes important again. If you want your sweater to measure 28" across the chest and there are 5 stitches per inch with the type of yarn you are using, you will need approximately 70 stitches on the front and back along with a couple of extra stitches for the seams. Check the pattern to see what size gives that number of stitches across the back.

Embroidery

A few embroidery stitches can be a great addition to a sweater—a spark of color as well as texture, a way to make a garment unique. Here is an explanation of the simple stitches we have included in some of the patterns in this book.

French Knot

This is the perfect stitch for little round things like apples or flowers in a field. Bring the yarn up through the sweater where you want the knot to be and wind the yarn around the needle 3 to 5 times close to the sweater. Then insert the needle close by and hold the twisted yarn with your thumb while you pull the needle gently all the way through to form a knot.

Outline Stitch

This is somewhat like a back stitch except that each stitch is started just beside and behind the end of the previous stitch, creating a heavier line.

Loop Stitch

Bring the yarn up through the sweater to form a loop and insert the needle close to the same spot. Then bring the needle back up to catch the other end of the loop.

Duplicate Stitch

Use this stitch to correct a mistake or to add a stitch in another color after the sweater is complete. Pull the needle up through the stitch below the one to be covered. Pass the needle under both sides of the stitch above the one to be covered and back down through the stitch where the yarn entered.

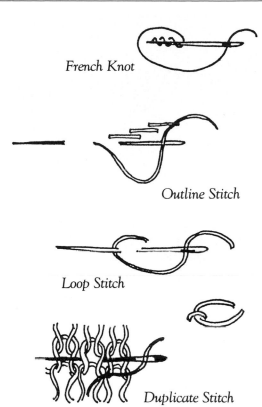

French Knot

Outline Stitch

Loop Stitch

Duplicate Stitch

Glossary of Terms

st, sts	stitch, stitches
K	knit
P	purl
st st	stockinette stitch
incr	increase
bet	between
dec	decrease
rnd	round
rem	remaining
oz	ounce
tog	together
K 2 tog	knit two stitches together
in	inch
approx	approximately
beg	beginning
MC	main color

10

Kids and Islands

Some things are different about raising children in a small town on an island. It starts with conception, as it does anywhere else, but here a pregnancy is very closely watched and much discussed (on an island, everything is much discussed). As soon as the pregnancy is made public—although many may have suspected it already—the child is counted as part of the prospective class of _____ . In a town where a class of one is not unheard of, every child has great social significance.

The future viability of an island is often measured by the health of its school. Without a healthy school—one with a sufficient number of children—many families would not want to stay. The population might then be insufficient to maintain the essential components of community life—a store, church, gas pumps, community organizations. With such lingering thoughts, a new baby in town can always be seen as a valuable addition.

The experience of childbirth itself is given a little extra drama when a trip to the mainland is part of the plan. Since the nearest hospital is 12 miles away by water which can be impassable in terrible weather, careful thought and planning must be given to an event that often defies planning. Some women choose to plant themselves on the mainland a short time prior to the due date, hoping that the baby will be timely and that a one week stay doesn't turn into six weeks. Others wait for those pangs of labor, often making a false trip or two when the pains don't result in the desired outcome. Occasionally there is the great drama—a baby feels a need to appear while the mother is still on the fifteen minute mail plane ride or worse yet (especially for the captain), on the one hour lobster boat ride. Fortunately, few tragedies have resulted and many wonderful stories evolve from these experiences that become a part of a baby's birthmark.

Once parents are given that title by the appearance of their baby, they are treated to an abundance of advice from people who have been keenly aware of the growing up of many. There is considerable common wisdom freely shared—wanted or not—that often provides a calming sense that you are not alone.

The real treat comes from the great awareness people have of the children around them. All babies are closely scrutinized and relatives several generations past can be seen in every face. Toddlers are watched on the ferry trip and someone is always ready to lend a hand if the ride gets rough. Most people have a smile for any child and are willing to engage in a bit of conversation as the children grow older. Adults are addressed on a first name basis and children from quite a young age learn to feel comfortable conversing with people of all ages.

Safety is not a major concern since the idea of strangers is a little foreign when almost everyone must enter the community through the very public ferry passage and there is no such thing as a quick escape. People naturally look out for the children. A group playing in a dangerous place or not being careful in a boat may well be reprimanded by the nearest adult.

On our island there isn't an abundance of organized activities. There is often a school play and every year there is basketball, but there aren't the endless lists of sports, musical experiences, clubs, and other activities commonplace to most of America. At first glance it may seem as if the children are not provided with enough outlets for their creative natures. Given another perspective, however, there are many benefits and, in fact, it is just a difference. Parents are not turned into chauffeurs and neighborhoods are not just a place to rest your head at night, but actually a place to play. In fact "play" is still a word that has meaning and children don't seem to grow up quite as fast; they don't need the tough edges of sophistication necessary to cope with rapid changes. Young kids still go into the woods and build "camps"; they go sledding and skating in the winter. Many children occasionally accompany their parents to their jobs, where they may observe work as a fact of life and the skills of their parents first hand—working in the woods, building a boat or stocking the shelves in the store.

As children move into high school the limitations of island life are more obvious—classes are small and the students stay with each other and often the same teachers for their whole school career. Socializing and traditional dating customs are somewhat confusing when you are with the same students you have known for years. On the other hand, in such a small system everyone who chooses to is allowed to participate and can make an impact. Kids organize fund raisers, plan trips, and make dances happen. Two kids can take control of the school yearbook and make major changes. Everyone gets to be in the school play and anyone who submits an article or drawing to the local newspaper is apt to get it published. It can be a wonderful thing to have your voice heard in an adult world and children on an island are given that voice.

In summer the pace of life changes for all of us, including the children. Their lives are filled with an abundance of activities to choose from—including jobs, swimming, tennis and sailing lessons, and just hanging around downtown to see what is going on. Younger kids hop on their bikes and ride to town for a visit to the candy counter while older kids "mess around" in boats and experience that wonderful sense of freedom of being able to rush away from or to something. There is also the influx of summer kids to provide new friends, summer crushes or just a diversity of faces to look at.

Although many of the children start to work at jobs such as babysitting, housecleaning, and mowing lawns when they are still quite young, they always seem to have time for fun. Downtown is the focus—watching the boats come and go, hanging around the burger shop, and best of all jumping off the high ferry landing into the cold ocean waters below.

When thinking about the qualities of life we would want to provide for children—safety, a rich life full with possibilities, a sense of security among people who care, a beautiful natural environment, a chance to be a part of a system where it's possible to make an impact—it's hard to imagine what we are missing.

Schoolbus—Front

Materials:
400 yds Royal Blue
150 yds Red
120 yds Green
20 yds Yellow
20 yds Purple
20 yds White
Directions Page 19

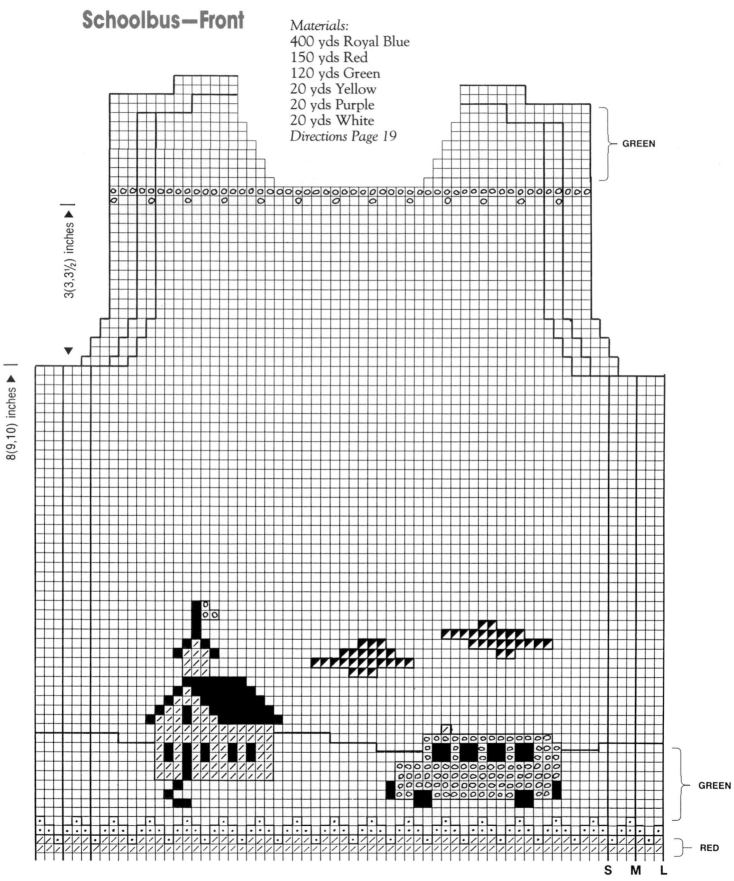

GREEN

3(3,3½) inches ▲ |

8(9,10) inches ▲ |

GREEN

RED

S M L

LEGEND: ■ = Purple. ⊡ = Yellow. ⧄ = Red. ⊡ = Blue. ⧄ = White.
All ribbings are worked in Red.

Schoolbus—Sleeve

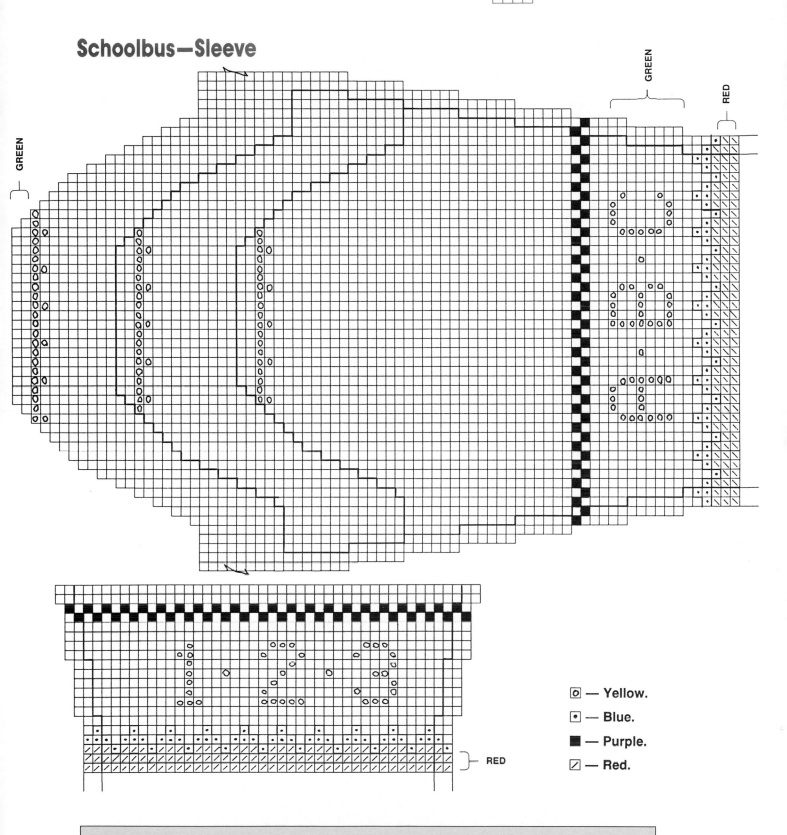

o — Yellow.

• — Blue.

■ — Purple.

⟋ — Red.

Winter always arrives with the cold winds and the blinding snow, often causing icy roads. On alot of cold, windy winter days the ferry doesn't run and the residents have to cancel all the plans that they had made. *Holly Parsons, Grade 9*

Schoolbus Pullover

Country Scene Pullover

Country Scene—Front

Materials:
400 yds Light Blue
150 yds Peach
160 yds Light Green
50 yds White
50 yds Dark Green
Directions Page 19

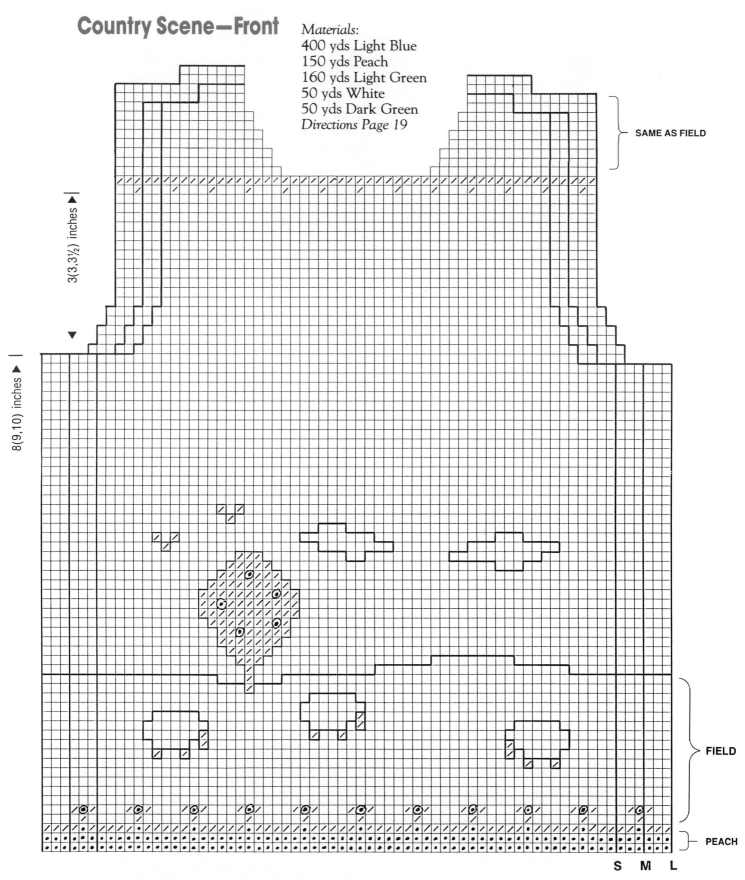

SAME AS FIELD

3(3,3½) inches ▲|

8(9,10) inches ▲|

FIELD

PEACH

S   M   L

☑ **Dark Green.**   ⊡ = **Peach.**   ⊙ = **French Knots are done in Peach.**
All ribbings and first two rows done in Peach.
Sheep & Clouds = White.   **Sky = Light Blue.**   **Field = Light Green.**

Country Scene—Sleeve

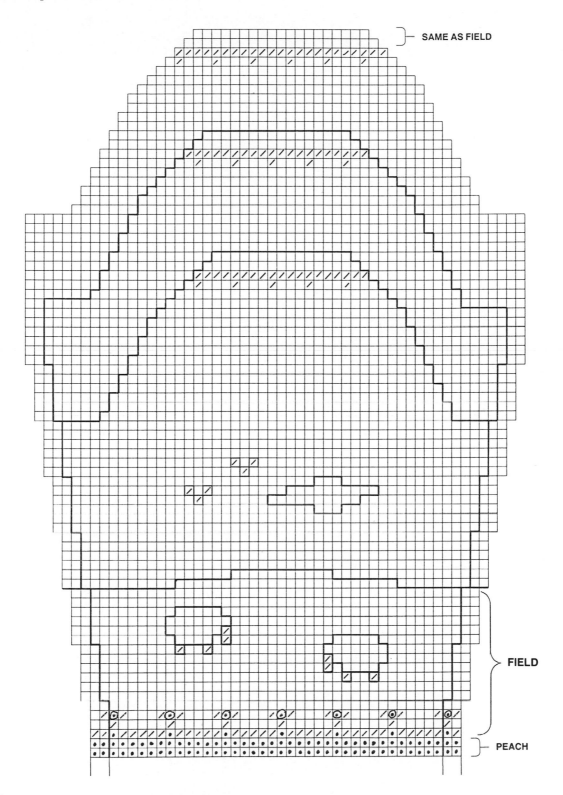

SAME AS FIELD

FIELD

PEACH

☑ Dark Green.

⊡ = Peach.   ⊙ = French Knots are done in Peach.

All ribbings and first two rows done in Peach.
Sheep & Clouds = White.   Sky = Light Blue.
Field = Light Green.

City Scene Pullover

Child Scenic Pullover

This pattern is used for Schoolbus, Country Scene, and City Scene.

Sizes: 2 (4, 6)
Needles: US 5 and 8—or whatever size needed to get stitch gauge of 5 sts = 1 in. using double strand Fingering Weight Wool.

Front

Using smaller needles and ribbing color, cast on 56 (62, 68) sts. Work K1, P1 ribbing for 2 in. Change to larger needles and follow chart. Work until piece measures 8 (9, 10) in or desired length to underarm.

Armholes: Bind off 4 (5, 5) sts beg next 2 rows. Dec 1 st each end every knit row 3 times. Work straight until armhole measures 3 (3, 3½) in. Work 2 rows as per chart.

Neck: Work 13 (15, 18) sts. Place rem sts on holder. Dec 1 st at neck edge every other row 4 times. Bind off at shoulder edge as per chart. Work other shoulder to correspond, leaving center 16 sts on holder.

Back

Work same shaping as front except neck. Bind off sts for shoulder and place 24 back neck sts on holder. Work lower borders the same as front and bring bands of background color around back to correspond with front.

Sleeves

Using smaller needles, cast on 36 (36, 40) sts and work K1, P1 ribbing for 2 in. Change to larger needles and follow chart, incr 1 st each side every 6th row 5 (7, 7) times. Total number of sts will be 46 (50, 54) sts.

Continue until sleeve measures 9 (11, 12) in or desired length to underarm.

Sleeve Cap: Bind off 4 (5, 5) sts beg next 2 rows. Dec 1 st each end every knit row 6 times, then 1 st each end every row 4 times. Work design and continue to dec 1 st each end every row 2 more times. Bind off remaining sts.

Finishing

Sew left shoulder seam. Using smaller needles and Color A, pick up and knit sts on holders and approx 9 (9, 10, 11) sts at each neck edge. Work K1, P1 ribbing for 1 in. Bind off very loosely, using a much larger needle. Sew remaining seams and weave in ends.

I would rather be on North Haven than New York. But why, you ask? You can not walk the beach with your best friend in New York, that's what. I like to see the sea gulls fly. No noise. Only me and my friend talking to each other. The water gets our feet wet as we walk by. There's no sand, all rocks, but I don't mind. We watch the boats fly by and the waves hit the rocks. Splash! We are so wet. We look at each other and laugh.

So many things to do on the beach on an island day. There are no better places than the island. There are so many places, but only one right for me. Only the island—small, quiet and fun. But there is no room—you are not moving in.

Cecily Pingree, Grade 4

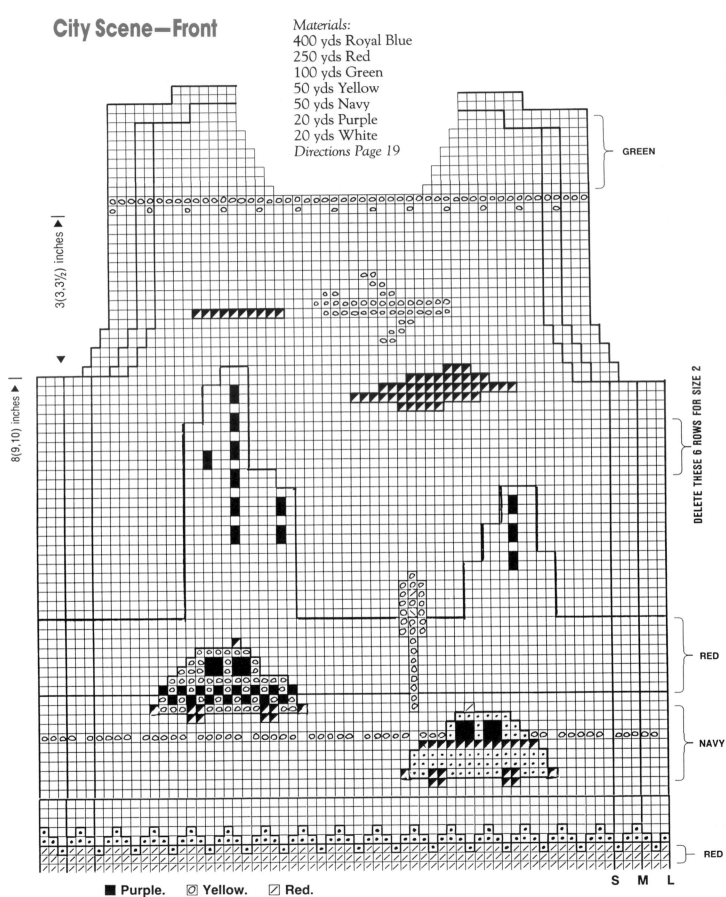

City Scene—Front

Materials:
400 yds Royal Blue
250 yds Red
100 yds Green
50 yds Yellow
50 yds Navy
20 yds Purple
20 yds White
Directions Page 19

GREEN

3(3,3½) inches ▲|

▼

8(9,10) inches ▲|

DELETE THESE 6 ROWS FOR SIZE 2

RED

NAVY

RED

S M L

■ **Purple.** ◫ **Yellow.** ⧄ **Red.**
⊡ **Blue.** ◪ **White.** ◺ **Green.**
All ribbings are worked in Red.

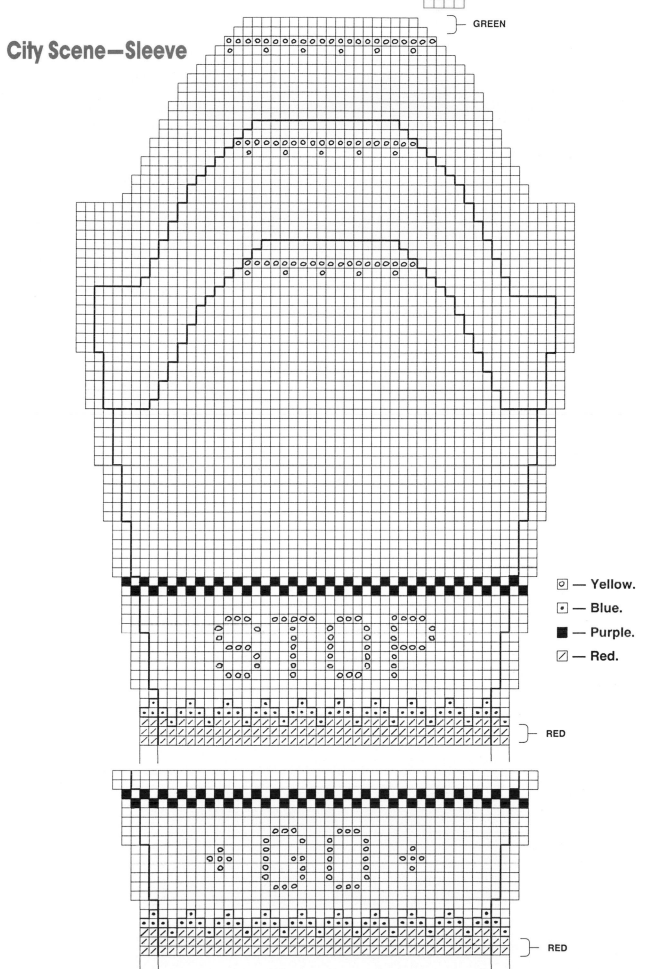

City Scene—Sleeve

GREEN

☑ — Yellow.

• — Blue.

■ — Purple.

☑ — Red.

RED

RED

Farmyard Cardigan

Child Scenic Cardigan

This pattern is used for Farmyard and Train.

Sizes: 4, 6, 8
Needles: 24 in circular needles. US sizes 5 and 7—or whatever size needed to get stitch gauge of 5 sts = 1 in.
Buttons: 5 Pewter Buttons
Sweater is worked in Cotton/Wool Blend

Body

Using smaller needles and White, cast on 132 (136, 144) sts. Work 6 rows in Garter Stitch (knit every row), change to Plum, knit 2 rows. Next row: Change to larger needles and start chart. Work chart in stockinette stitch until correct length to armhole.

Armholes: Work 30 (30, 32) sts, bind off 6 (8, 8) sts, work 60 (60, 64) sts, bind off 6 (6, 8) sts, and work rem 30 (30, 32) sts. Next row: Attach new balls of yarn where needed and work back across. Dec 1 st at each armhole edge every other row four times. Work till armhole measures 3½ (4, 4½) in.

Neck: With right-side facing, bind off 8 sts at neck edge beg next 2 rows. Dec 1 st at each neck edge every knit row 4 times. Work shoulders as per chart. Place shoulder sts on holders to be knit tog.

Sleeves

Cast on 40 (40, 44) sts using White and smaller needle. Work 6 rows in Garter Stitch (knit every row); change to Plum, knit 2 rows; change to sky color, and work sleeve in Stockinette Stitch using larger needles, as per chart. Only left sleeve will have a "sun" on it. Press sleeve pieces.

Shoulders

Place front and back shoulder-pieces right-sides tog and using a third needle, knit tog 1 st from front and 1 st from back then bind off sts until no sts remain. Leave back neck sts on holder to be picked up when doing trim. Press body.

Trim

Using smaller needles and White yarn, with right-side facing and starting at lower corner of left front, pick up and knit available sts on edge of White trim, attach ball of Plum, pick up and knit approx 3 out of every 4 sts up the front; cast on 1 st at corner; pick up and knit 3 out of 4 sts around curve of neck; knit back neck sts from holder; then knit 3 out of 4 sts on next curve; cast on 1 st at corner, and knit 3 out of 4 sts down other front to lower trim, attach ball of White and pick up and knit sts on edge of White. Knit one more row in Plum. Change to White and knit one row, adding 1 st each side of corner st. Knit second row. Knit third row while adding 1 st each side of corner sts. Knit fourth row in White and work button-holes as follows: Count number of sts between corners of right-front for girls, left-front for boys. Allowing 2 sts at top, 3 sts at bottom, and 2 sts each for 5 buttonholes (total of 15 sts), divide rem sts by 4 to find number of sts between buttonholes. Any sts left over should be put at bottom. (Example— total sts=86: K2, bind off 2, K17, bind off 2, K17, bind off 2, K17, bind off 2, K17, bind off 2, K6). Also this row: Dec 5 sts evenly around curve of neck. Knit 5th row and cast on 2 sts over bound-off sts for buttonholes and incr 1 st each side of corner sts. Knit 6th row. In 7th row, bind off loosely using a larger needle.

Finishing

Sew sleeve seams, right-sides tog, using back stitch. Turn body wrong-side-out. Slip left sleeve into left armhole and carefully stitch so that "sun" looks fairly together. Sew in right sleeve. Weave in ends. Sew on buttons.

My favorite thing about the Ferry. I like the ferry because it brings all the cars and my car too.
Tess Haskell, Grade 1

Farmyard Cardigan

Materials:
500 yds Light Green
150 yds White
150 yds Dark Green
60 yds Plum

20 yds Red
20 yds Yellow
20 yds Brown
10 yds Pink
Directions Page 23

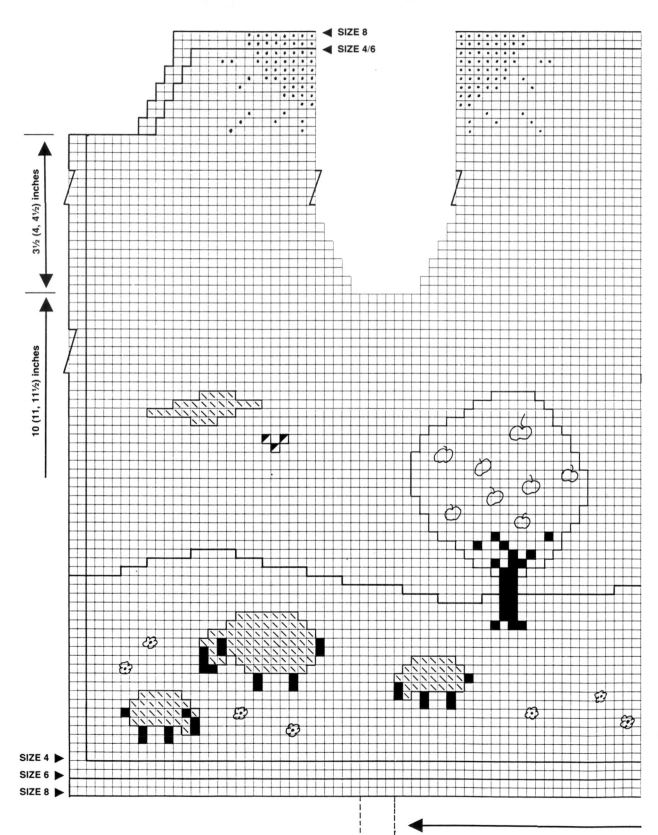

◄ SIZE 8
◄ SIZE 4/6

3½ (4, 4½) inches

10 (11, 11½) inches

SIZE 4 ►
SIZE 6 ►
SIZE 8 ►

- ⊡ = **Yellow.**
- ◪ = **Plum.**
- ⊠ = **Red.**
- ◼ = **Brown.**
- ◺ = **White.**

- ❀ = **Pink (French Knots).**
- ◔ = **Red (French Knots).**
- **Field** = **Dark Green.**
- **Foliage** = **Dark Green.**
- **Sky** = **Light Green-Blue.**

■ = KNIT ROW

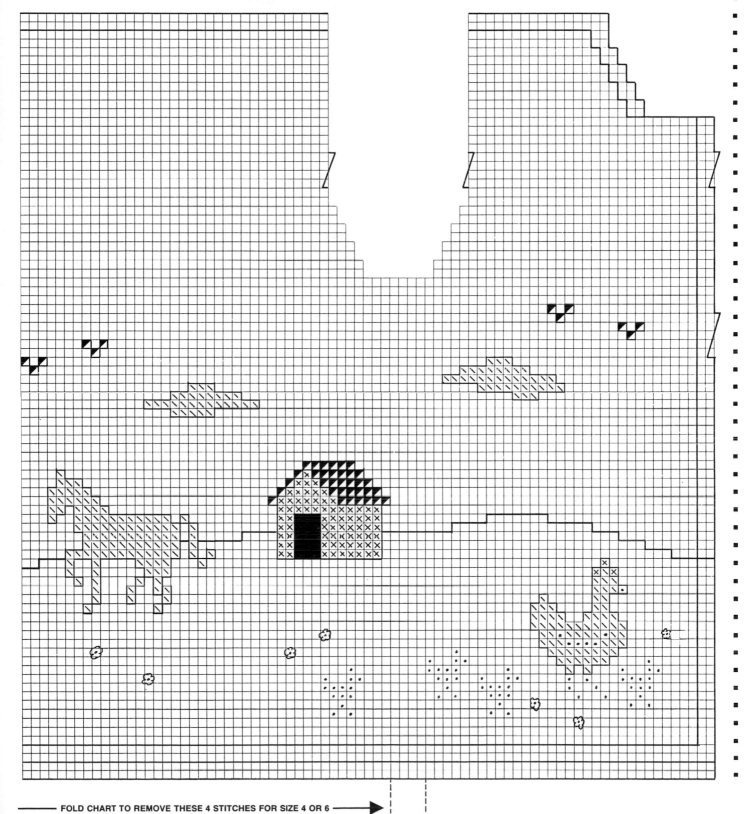

← **FOLD CHART TO REMOVE THESE 4 STITCHES FOR SIZE 4 OR 6** →

Farmyard and Train—Sleeve

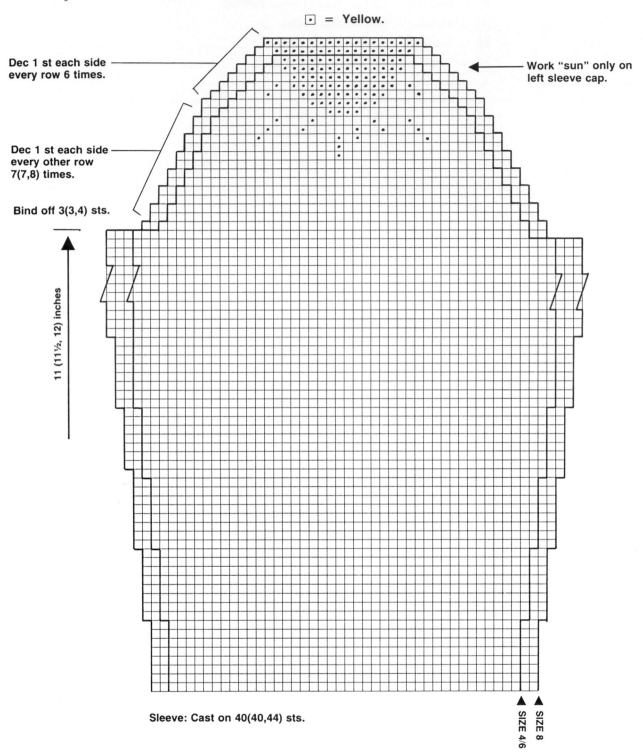

☐ = Yellow.

Dec 1 st each side every row 6 times.

Work "sun" only on left sleeve cap.

Dec 1 st each side every other row 7(7,8) times.

Bind off 3(3,4) sts.

11 (11½, 12) inches

Sleeve: Cast on 40(40,44) sts.

SIZE 4/6

SIZE 8

hen I first moved to the island I thought it was going to be boring and my brother thought it was going to be boring because there wouldn't be any video arcades. When we got here we found out it was pretty nice. I love the island because we don't have to worry about traffic jams. *Siri Anderson, Grade 4*

Train Cardigan

Train Cardigan

Materials:
500 yds Blue
150 yds Green
150 yds White
75 yds Purple

40 yds Yellow
30 yds Dark Blue
20 yds Red
20 yds Dark Green
Directions Page 23

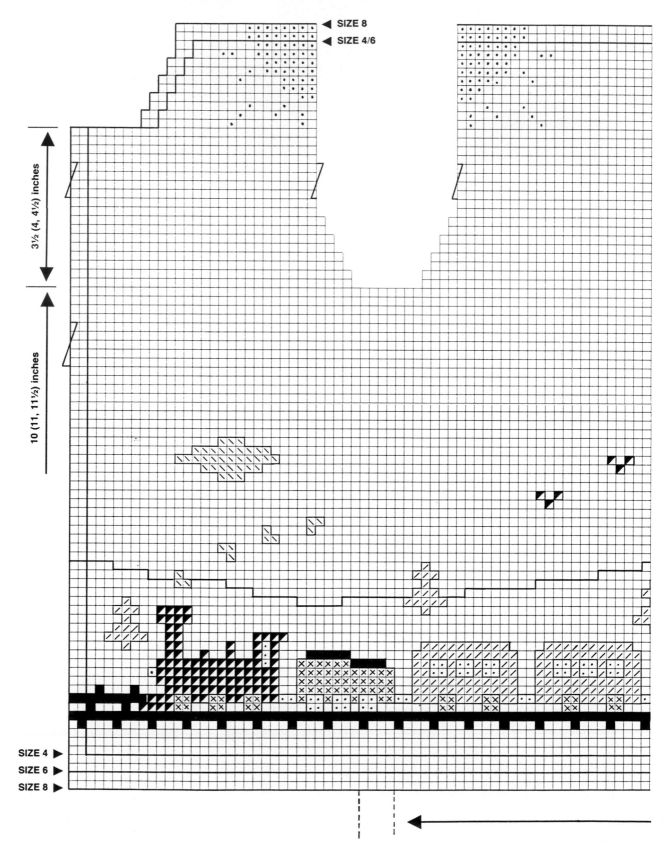

⊡ = Yellow.   ◳ = White.

▨ = Plum.   ◺ = Dark Green.

⊠ = Red.   Field = Light Green.

■ = Dark Blue.   Sky = Light Blue.

= KNIT ROW

◄ FOLD CHART TO REMOVE THESE 4 STITCHES FOR SIZE 4 OR 6 ➤

Child Care That Involves Everybody

Child care has become a problem everywhere and this community is no exception. Single parenting or the need for two incomes has put most women in the workplace, with their children in need of a place to be. In earlier times, members of extended families were available to assist with this task, or non-working mothers took over this role by taking in a few extra children; both are less common today. In our community a group of women with children of preschool age are trying cooperative child care.

By using the building of the local American Legion Post and dividing the week into shifts, the mothers managed to organize a system that accommodated their needs. Parents work one or two shifts, based on the number of days their child is in the group. The organization of this structure involved hours of discussion as details regarding discipline, appropriate snacks, and other concerns were worked out.

The routine includes all of the wonderful fare that goes into a child's day—lots of coloring, books to read, snacks to be eaten (and all those spills). The toys are all donated and serious sharing is involved for the child who used to know the toy intimately. Because there are so many people involved, written instructions and lists are found everywhere: Practical lists with instructions on running the furnace, the children's own list of acts that constitute misbehavior (such as biting, jumping on the couch and letting go of the rope when on a walk), and a long list so that nothing is forgotten as the day ends. Of course this last list covers all of the usual—turn off the furnace, sweep up, put away the toys, and most important (so there are no surprises in the morning) empty the potty chair.

The women who are involved learn much about the art of compromise and working together and there are true opportunities for sharing child rearing techniques in subtle ways as your shift mate handles a situation. For the children there are the hidden securities of being embraced by the many members of the community who participate in their care.

Two mornings a week the "Sea Urchins" nursery school is run in the same location by a dedicated community member who started it years ago. The child care mothers bring any under age babies to their homes while the teacher and her helper provide a beginning for the school experience which is around the corner. Sitting up at a table, listening to a story, and working on an art project introduce new skills. Occasional walks on the beach, rides on the fire truck, and a graduation (complete with diplomas for everyone and black paper hats) become part of the island traditions young children look forward to.

These are the early stages of development of tomorrow's community. The children will one day be the teenagers in our town, playing on the basketball team and sometimes getting into trouble. They are our neighbors' children, and we are helping to make them feel more secure in their environment. We are able to be involved in a very intimate way with these future adults—those who will run the community systems when we grow tired of the job. It is one more way a small town looks after its present and future.

Summertime Vest

Versatile Vest

This pattern is used for Summertime, Appletree with Sheep, and Camden Hills.

Sizes: 6 (8, 10, 12)
Needles: US 4 and 7—or whatever size needed to get a stitch gauge of 5 sts = 1 in 24 in circular #4 needle for neck

Front

Using smaller needles and MC, cast on 68 (72, 76, 80) sts. Work in K1, P1 ribbing for 18 rows. At the end of last row of ribbing, incr 1 st [69 (73, 77, 81) sts]. Change to larger needles.

Row 1 (and all right-side rows except cable rows): K8 (10, 12, 14), P2, K4, P2, K2, work chart on next 33 sts, K2, P2, K4, P2, K8 (10, 12, 14).

Row 2 (and all wrong side rows): P8 (10, 12, 14), K2, P4, K2, P2, work chart on next 33 sts, P2, K2, P4, K2, P8 (10, 12, 14).

Row 3 (and every 6th row): K8 (10, 12, 14), P2, C4b (do this by slipping 2 sts to a double-pointed needle, hold in back of work, K2, K2 sts from dp needle), P2, K2, work chart (33 sts), K2, P2, C4b, P2, K8 (10, 12, 14). Continue in this manner until piece measures 11 (11½, 12, 12½) in or desired length to underarm.

Armholes: Bind off 4 (5, 6, 7) sts beg next 2 rows. Dec 1 st each end every knit row 3 (4, 5, 6) times. When chart is completed work neck shaping as follows: Work 2 rows MC. Next row: Work 16 sts, place next 25 sts on holder, attach another ball of MC yarn, work 16 sts. On right side, dec 1 st each side at neck edge every row 4 times (12 sts rem on each side). Continue working cables until armhole measures 5½ (6, 6, 6½) in. Bind off.

Back

Work same as front except work center 33 sts in stockinette stitch using MC.

Finishing

When back and front are completed, sew tog at shoulders matching sts. Using a 24 in circular #4 needle, pick up and knit every available st plus sts on holders, around neck. Work 3 rows ribbing (K1, P1). Bind off using a larger needle. Sew side seams. Work ribbing around armholes to match neck. Weave in ends.

Summer is the best time of year. I start sailing in June. I think it's the most fun sport for the summer. I like to capsize the boat. It's alot of fun sailing over the ferry boat waves. I hate to bail out the boat. By the time you finish it seems like a whole year went by. Every day I wear my swim suit so I can swim after sailing lessons. I like to race sail boats on Saturday. *Nick White, Grade 4*

My life is very simple. In the summer I like to lobster in my new boat. I also do ferry trips by taking people across the thorofare. I don't have very much free time because I am always working. When the water is rough and I can't use my boat I just stay in the boat shop and work. In other places you might not find kids lobstering. That's why I like living on an island. *Jacob Brown, Grade 5*

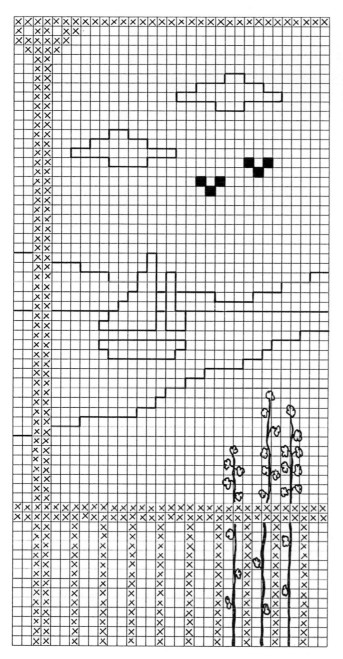

Summertime Vest

*Sweater is worked in Cotton/Wool Blend
Materials:*
2 (2, 3, 3)3 ½ oz skeins Main Color
50 yds Green
50 yds Blue
25 yds Lavender
5 yds each Pink, Yellow and Blue
Directions Page 32

Clouds & Sailboat = White.

Hills & Birds = Medium Green.

Sky & Water = Blue.

Field = Light Green.

Porch Railing = Main Color or White.

Flowers = French Knots, worked in Yellow, Pink & Blue. Flower Stalks are Dark Green Outline Stitch.

he island that I live on reminds me of a whole different world. In one way it reminds me of a lonely place where no one is and in another way it tells me that everyone respects each other. Everyone knows one another here. Many people are related to each other. There is not one moment when one person doesn't wave or say a friendly hello. The island can be boring sometimes. A car passes every once in a while but nothing really happens until summer. The island lights up on special occasions such as the fourth of July and in the summer when many people are here. *Susan Joyce, Grade 8*

Appletree with Sheep Vest

Camden Hills Vest

Appletree with Sheep Vest

Sweater is worked in Knitting
Worsted Weight Wool
Materials:
2 (4oz) skeins Main Color
50 yds Light Green
50 yds Light Blue
20 yds Natural White
20 yds Dark Sheeps Gray
10 yds Dark Green
5 yds Red
5 yds Yellow
Directions Page 32

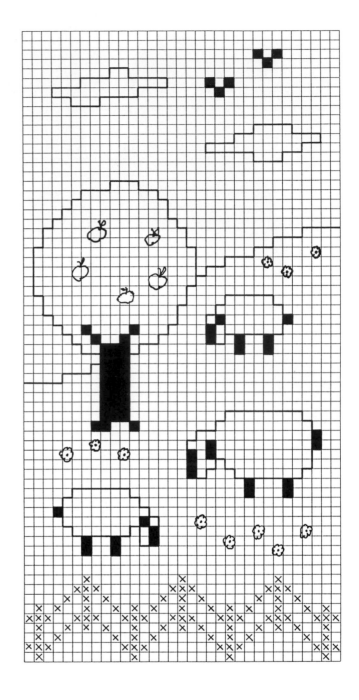

Clouds & Sheep = White.

Hill = Pale Green.

Tree Foliage = Dark Green.

Fence = Main Color.

Sky = Blue.

Apples = Red (French Knots).

Flowers = Yellow (French Knots).

■ = Brown.

⊠ = purl on knit side, knit on purl side.

---

ike Riding

I like to go bike riding alot in the summer to the beach. There are alot of small hills before I reach Apple Tree Hill. It's very hard to go up Apple Tree Hill because it is very steep and big. When I reach the beach I go swimming. When I get out of the water I start heading home on my bike. When I reach Apple Tree Hill again I go like a lightning bolt down it! It's hard going up, but it's really fun going down.
David Boshko, Grade 2

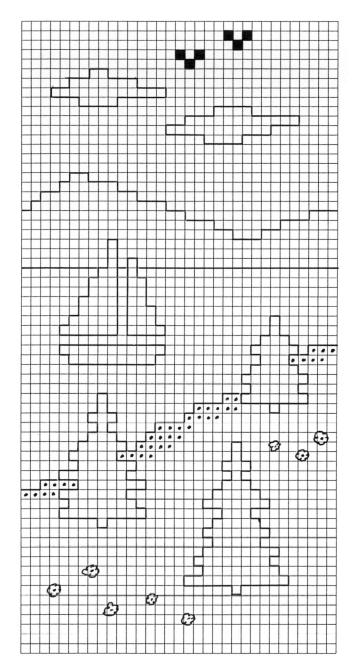

Camden Hills Vest

Sweater is worked in Knitting Worsted Weight Wool
Materials:
2 (4oz) skeins Main Color
50 yds Light Heather for Sky
30 yds Blue
20 yds Lavender
20 yds Dark Green
20 yds Natural White
Directions Page 32

Clouds & Sailboat = White.

Trees & Birds = Dark Green.

Hills = Purple.

Sky = Light Heather.

Field = Main Color.

Water = Blue.

Flowers in field are French Knots worked in Sky Color.

⊠ = **purl on knit side, knit on purl side.**

I like North Haven because there's alot of peace and quiet. One of my favorite things to do in the summer is sailing. You turn the tiller one way and the boat goes the opposite. Everyone who takes sailing lessons knows that. Sometimes I hate it on rough days. Once on a rough day the rudder fell off and I was going around in circles because I had the wrong rudder for my boat.

We had a race once but Nick got all of the wind and won. People bumped into each other alot. North Haven is my favorite place to be and I never want to leave here. *Jamien Shields, Grade 4*

Sailboat Pullover

Youth Cable Pullover

This pattern is used for Sheep in a Meadow Pullover, Appletree Pullover, Sailboat Pullover and Seagull Pullover.

Sizes : 6 (8, 10, 12)
Needles: US 4 and 7—or whatever size needed to get stitch gauge of 5 sts = 1 in using Knitting Worsted Yarn.

Front

Using smaller needles, cast on 66 (69, 72, 75) sts. Work K2, P1 ribbing for 2½ in. Incr 0 (1, 2, 3) sts evenly across last row of ribbing [66 (70, 74, 78) sts]. Change to larger needles and proceed as follows:

Rows 1, 3: K8 (10, 12, 14), P2, K4, P2, K4, P2, K22, P2, K4, P2, K4, P2, K8 (10, 12, 14).

Rows 2, 4: P8 (10, 12, 14), K2, P4, K2, P4, K2, P22, K2, P4, K2, P4, K2, P8 (10, 12, 14).

Row 5: K8 (10, 12, 14), P2, C4b (do this by slipping 2 sts to holder, hold in back of work, K2, K2 from holder), P2, C4b, P2, K22, P2, C4f (slip 2 sts to holder, hold in front of work, K2, K2 from holder), P2, C4f, P2, K8 (10, 12, 14).

Rows 6, 8, 10: Same as 2.
Rows 7, 9: Same as 1.
Row 11: Same as 5.

Continue repeating rows 1 and 2 with no more cabling until work measures 8 (9, 9½, 10) in or 2 in less than desired length to underarm. This is the measurement that will determine the length of sweater. Finished sweater length using these measurements is 10 (11, 11½, 12) in. Any adjustments should be made now. Repeat rows 5-11, then rows 2 and 3 once. With wrong side facing you, knit next three rows to create 2 ridges on right side and then start chart.

Armholes: Bind off 2 (3, 3, 5) sts beg next 2 rows, [62 (64, 68, 68) sts]. Dec 1 st each end every knit row 3 (3, 4, 4) times. Continue following chart until neck opening is reached.

Neck: On right side, work 20 (21, 22, 22) sts. Place rem sts on holder. Dec 1 st every other row at neck edge 3 (3, 4, 4) times. Bind off 5 (6, 6, 6) sts at shoulder edge once, bind off 6 sts twice. Work other side to correspond, leaving center 16 neck sts on holder.

Back

Work same as front except neck. Do not follow charted design but rather work stockinette stitch above ridges. Work armholes and shoulders to correspond to front, leaving center 22 (22, 24, 24) back neck sts on holder.

Sleeves

Using smaller needles, cast on 36 (36, 39, 42) sts. Work in K2, P1 ribbing for 2½ (2½, 3) in; incr 0 (2, 1, 0) sts in last row ribbing. Change to larger needles and establish sleeve cables as follows:

Row 1: K11 (12, 13, 14), P2, K4, P2, K4, P2, K11 (12, 13, 14). Continue working the cables as for front and back, rows 1-11, while incr 1 st each end every 6th row 6 times. Work until sleeve measures 10 (11, 12, 13) in or 2 in less than desired length of sleeve to underarm. Work cables again (pattern rows 5-11). Work rows 2 and 3 once. Knit next 3 rows to form 2 ridges.

Sleeve Cap: Bind off 2 (3, 3, 5) sts beg next 2 rows. Dec 1 st each end every knit row until 24 (22, 22, 20) sts rem. Bind off 3 sts beg next 4 rows. Bind off rem 12 (10, 10, 8) sts.

Finishing

Sew left shoulder seam. Using smaller needles, pick up and knit sts on holders and approx 9 (9, 10, 11) sts at each neck edge. Work in ribbing of K2, P1 for 1 in. Bind off very loosely using a much larger needle. Sew rem seams and weave in ends.

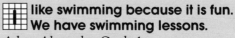 like swimming because it is fun. We have swimming lessons.
Adam Alexander, Grade 1

Sailboat Pullover

Materials:
3 (3, 4, 4) 4oz skeins Main Color
100 yds Sky Blue
2 yds Boat Color
20 yds Green
Directions Page 39

Size 12 —
Size 10 —
Sizes 6, 8 —

▢ White.

■ Dark.

◺ Green

☒ Purl on knit side, knit on purl side.

12 10 8 6

6 8 10 12

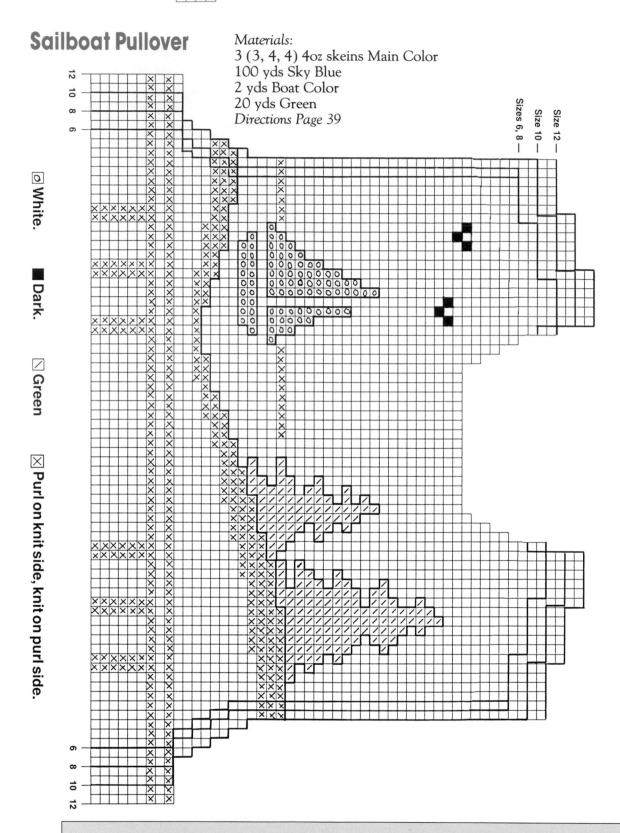

I have a special place I like to go. It's a beach called the Cubbyhole. My sister and I found alot of arrowheads, knives and a little cooking place. I like it because it's peaceful there and no noise. *Corey Beverage, Grade 3*

Sailboat Cardigan

Materials List Page 40
Directions Page 43

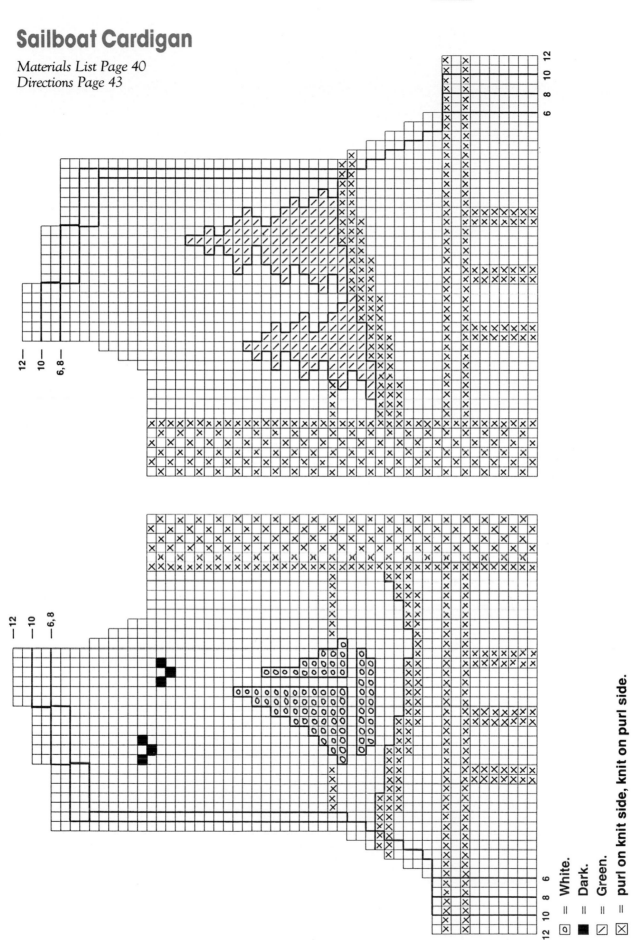

○ = White.
■ = Dark.
╱ = Green.
☒ = purl on knit side, knit on purl side.

Sheep in the Meadow Cardigan and Pullover

Youth Cable Cardigan

This pattern is used for Sheep in a Meadow Cardigan, Appletree Cardigan, and Sailboat Cardigan.

Sizes: 6 (8, 10, 12)
Needles: US 4 and 7—or whatever size needed to get stitch gauge of 5 sts = 1 in using Knitting Worsted Yarn.

Back

Using smaller needles cast on 66 (69, 72, 75) sts. Work K2, P1 ribbing for 2½ in; incr 0 (1, 2, 3) sts evenly across last row of ribbing [66 (70, 74, 78) sts]. Change to larger needles and proceed as follows:

Rows 1, 3: K8 (10, 12, 14), P2, K4, P2, K4, P2, K22, P2, K4, P2, K4, P2, K8 (10, 12, 14).

Rows 2, 4: P8 (10, 12, 14), K2, P4, K2, P4, K2, P22, K2, P4, K2, P4, K2, P8, (10, 12, 14).

Row 5: K8, (10, 12, 14), P2, C4b (do this by slipping 2 sts to holder, hold in back of work, K2, K2 from holder), P2, C4b, P2, K22, P2, C4f (slip 2 sts to holder, hold in front of work, K2, K2 from holder), P2, C4f, P2, K8 (10, 12, 14).

Rows 6, 8, 10: Same as 2.
Rows 7, 9: Same as 1.
Row 11: Same as 5.

Continue repeating rows 1 and 2 with no more cabling until work measures 8 (9, 9½, 10) in or 2 in less than desired length to underarm. This is the measurement that will determine the length of the sweater. Finished sweater length using these measurements is 10 (11, 11½, 12) in. Any adjustments should be made now. Repeat rows 5-11 then rows 2 and 3 once. With wrong side facing you, knit the next 3 rows to create 2 ridges on right side. The rest of the back is worked in stockinette stitch.

Armholes: Bind off 2 (3, 3, 5) sts beg next 2 rows [62 (64, 68, 68) sts]. Dec 1 st each end every knit row 3 (3, 4, 4) times. Work 29 (29, 29, 31) more rows. Bind off 5 (6, 6, 6) sts beg next 2 rows; bind off 6 sts beg next 4 rows. Place rem 22 (22, 24, 24) back neck sts on holder.

Directions are for girl's cardigan. Work buttonholes on left front for boy's cardigan.

Left Front

Using smaller needles cast on 35 (38, 41, 41) sts. Work K2, P1 ribbing on first 30 (33, 36, 36) sts, then seed stitch (K1, P1, K1, P1, K1) on rem 5 sts. Next row: K1, P1, K1, P1, K1 first 5 sts, then K1, P2 across row. Continue in ribbing to match back, then incr 3 (2, 1, 3) sts evenly across last row ribbing. Change to larger needles, K10 (12, 14, 16), P2, K4, P2, K4, P2, K8, P1, K1, P1, K1, P1, K1. Work cables same as back and continue front, keeping 5 sts in seed stitch for button band. When ridges are completed, start chart for left front.

Armhole: Bind off 2 (4, 4, 6) sts at beg next row. Dec 1 st at armhole edge every knit row 5 (4, 5, 5) times. Continue following chart until neck opening is reached. Place 11 sts at neck edge on holder, finish row. Dec 1 st at neck edge every knit row 3 times. Bind off shoulders as per chart.

Right Front

Work same as left front, only a mirror image, and work 6 buttonholes evenly spaced on button band. To work button-hole: Work to within 4 sts of end of row, bind off 2 sts firmly, finish row. On next row, K1, P1, and then cast on 2 sts firmly to make buttonhole. The first buttonhole should be halfway up ribbing; the last one should be midway in neck ribbing and the others spaced evenly between.

Continued Page 76

After dad and I played cribbage we went lobstering. The first traps had six lobsters but four were too small. The next haul was better than the first but we got tired and went to Dogfish Island and got some lunch. *Jeremiah MacDonald, Grade 5*

Sheep in the Meadow Pullover

Materials:
3 (3, 4, 4) 4oz skeins Main Color
20 yds White or Medium Gray depending
on whether you have chosen a light or dark
background
20 yds Dark Sheeps Gray
Directions Page 39

Size 12 —
Size 10 —
Sizes 6, 8 —

◧ White.

■ Dark.

☒ Purl on knit side, knit on purl side.

Sheep in the Meadow Cardigan

For Materials List see Page 44
Directions Page 43

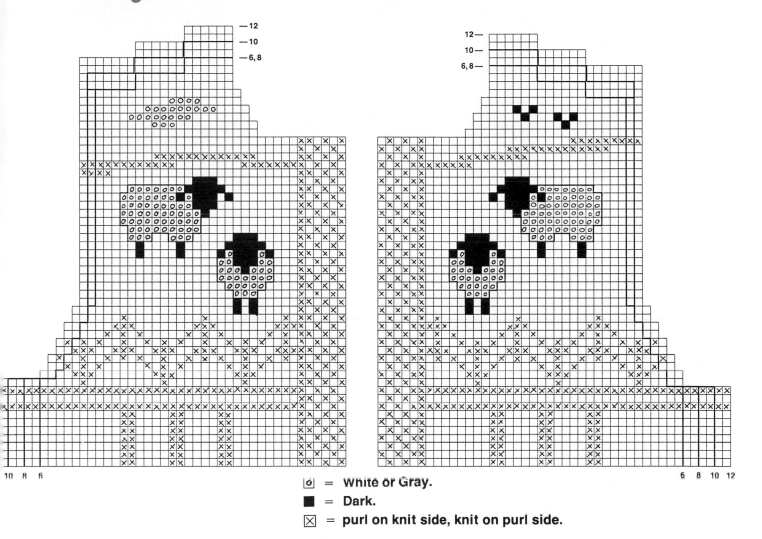

○ = White or Gray.
■ = Dark.
⊠ = purl on knit side, knit on purl side.

W hen you walk into a small classroom and you know everyone including the teacher, on such a personal scale, you get a sense of smallness but also a sense of togetherness.

There are so many other ways you notice you live on an island. One of them is downtown—a place where a kid growing up spends part of his or her life. A place where you notice the business of the summer and the peacefulness of the winter. A place full of new faces, welcome and not welcome, friend and enemy.

In the summer you notice even more that you live on an island in one sense—and in another sense you notice even less. This is because in the summertime with all the new stores, new summer residents and new tourists you don't feel isolated at all. But in the summer when you are out sailing or swimming off the ferry pier you again get a feeling of community and friends. *Hannah Pingree, Grade 7*

Appletree Cardigan

Appletree Cardigan

Materials List Page 48
Directions Page 43

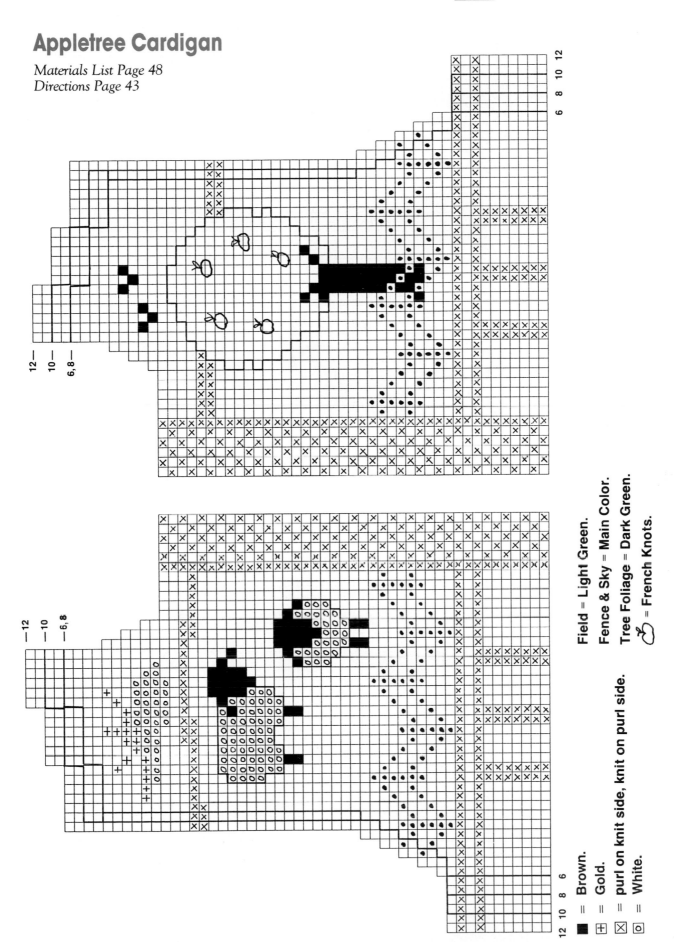

Field = Light Green.

Fence & Sky = Main Color.

Tree Foliage = Dark Green.

🍎 = French Knots.

■ = Brown.

✢ = Gold.

☒ = purl on knit side, knit on purl side.

◯ = White.

Appletree Pullover

Materials:
3 (3, 4, 4) 4oz skeins Main Color
20 yds White
20 yds Dark Sheeps Gray
20 yds Dark Green
75 yds Light Green
3 yds Yellow
3 yds Red
Directions Page 39

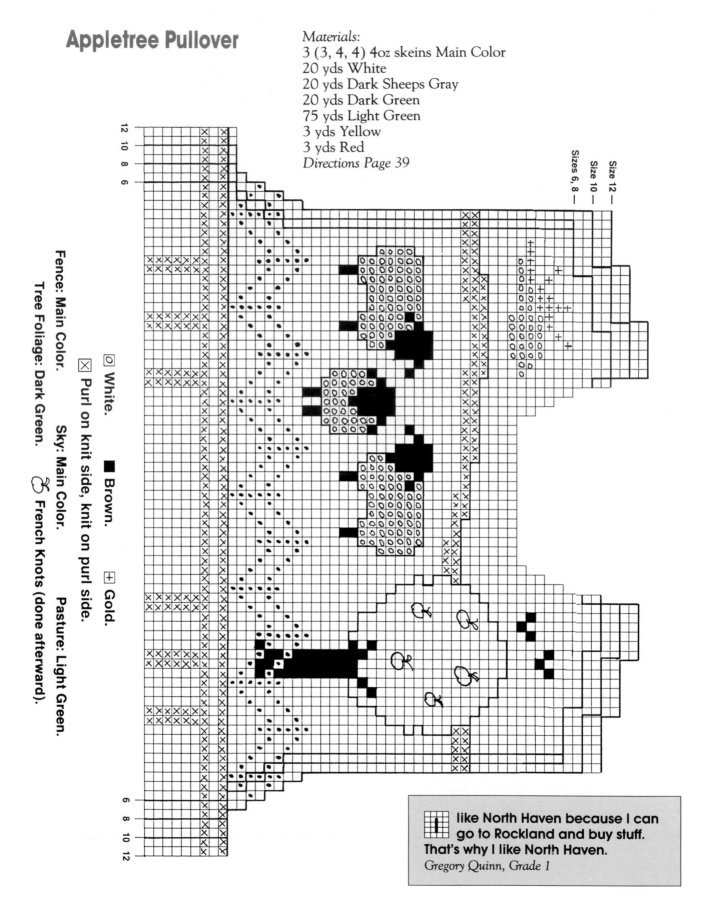

Fence: Main Color.   **Sky:** Main Color.   **Pasture:** Light Green.

Tree Foliage: Dark Green.

⊙ White.   ■ Brown.   ⊞ Gold.

⊠ Purl on knit side, knit on purl side.

ℰ French Knots (done afterward).

> I like North Haven because I can
> go to Rockland and buy stuff.
> **That's why I like North Haven.**
> *Gregory Quinn, Grade 1*

Basketball

Watching a basketball game, the one competitive sport our high school is involved in, gives a feeling of the spirit resting just under the surface of our community. Usually a boys' game and a girls' game are played on the same evening in the community gymnasium. If we are playing our staunch rival (the neighboring island), you need to arrive very early to get a seat or even a place to stand. The one set of bleachers and folding chairs set up in the small margin all around the gym allow a spectator to catch a stray ball occasionally and pitch it back into the game.

None of the spectators dress up but the coaches (whom you normally see in their work clothes) may be in a dress or suit and tie. An ex-coach begins the game with an announcement over the loudspeaker, "Good evening sports fans, welcome to the North Haven Auditorium for more exciting class D basketball action with the Rangeley Lakers versus the North Haven Hawks." We all love the unnecessarily grand announcement. The team runs out and the fans cheer and another night of basketball has begun.

With so few players, we are basically a one sport town. Having a basketball team takes a consistent and faithful effort on the part of the students, the school, and many members of the community. It is the one chance students have for a team sport experience and it is the one chance the community has to be faithful spectators.

Advice is abundant and the empathy of relatives and friends seems deeply intertwined with past experiences. Many wonderful and painful memories must be relived and the flavor of the game is heightened by the presence of players and coaches of yesteryear.

For a visiting team, playing on our island is often a unique experience. There is no packing into the school bus at the end of the game for the ride home—the last ferry has tied up for the night. All of the visiting students stay at the players' homes. This is a new twist on the traditional highly competitive relationship—how much can you hate or fear an opposing team member when he or she is spending the night in your house, sharing thoughts on the game and other matters with you.

For our students, traveling to "away" games gives an opportunity to visit other families and communities throughout the state. Teams are so small that eighth graders are a part of the "varsity" squad, so by twelfth grade such experiences have become familiar.

How do our teams do? People are always delighted to have a successful team, but the question more often is—will there be enough members for a team? There are years when there are not, and often, with only five members, no one can afford to foul out. There are however, some very exciting years when the team travels to the state tournaments. These games are broadcast on the radio, and the entire community participates as the team faces its largest crowds.

Kids start out in "Pee Wee" basketball in 4th grade which culminates every season with the mother/daughter game. Anticipating this, I began playing in the Sunday night women's games, hoping to learn some of the rules. The "alumni" (often called the "old ladies") get together and play the high school girls to keep them in practice. Since I grew up in another place during a generation when sports for girls weren't emphasized, this public display of my lack of knowledge or skill has been a little embarrassing, but a wonderful opportunity to face a different part of myself.

Seagull Pullover

Seagull Pullover

Sweater is worked in Cotton/Wool Blend
Materials:
4 (4, 5, 5) 3½ oz skeins Main Color
100 yds Sky Color
30 yds White
Directions Page 39

Work one row in white
mid-way in neck ribbing.

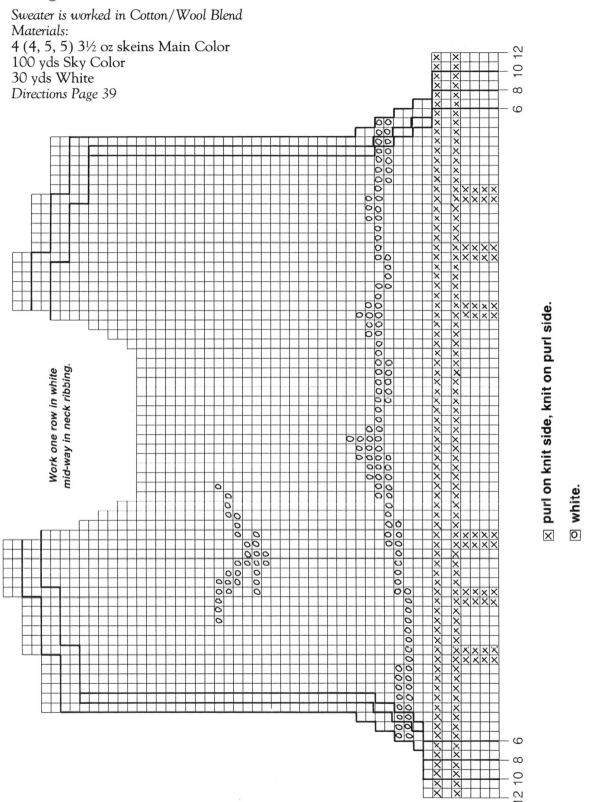

⊠ **purl on knit side, knit on purl side.**

◎ **white.**

Youth Chicken Pullover

Sizes: 6 (8, 10, 12)

Needles: US 4 and 7—or whatever size needed to get stitch gauge of 5 sts = 1 in using Knitting Worsted Yarn.

Materials:

3 (3, 4, 4) 4oz. skeins Main Color

10 yds each White and Brown Tweed

5 yds each Red, Yellow, and Dark Brown

Note:

The kernels of corn may be done in Duplicate Stitch or French Knots after completion. The chicken legs should be done in a dark color if you have chosen a light background, and in Yellow if your background is dark.

Front

Using smaller needles, cast on 66 (69, 72, 75) sts. Work K2, P1 ribbing for 2½ (2½, 3, 3) in, incr 1 (2, 3, 4) sts evenly across last row of ribbing. Change to larger needles and follow chart for front with chicken-wire pattern. Work until 10 (11, 11½, 12) in or desired length to underarm. End right side. With wrong side facing you, knit next 3 rows to form 2 ridges on right side of work.

Armholes: Bind off 3 (4, 4, 5) sts beg next 2 rows. Also work design. Dec 1 st each end every knit row 3 (3, 4, 4) times. Work until neck opening is reached. On right side, work 18 (19, 20, 21) sts. Place rem sts on holder. Dec 1 st every other row at neck edge 3 (3, 4, 4) times. Follow chart, bind off sts for shoulder as follows: Bind off 5 (6, 5, 6) sts beg next row. Then bind off 5 (5, 6, 6) sts beg next row and 5 sts last row. Work other side to correspond, leaving center 19 sts on holder.

Back

Work same as front until armhole. Continue chicken-wire instead of following chart. Work armholes same as front and continue to shoulders. Bind off sts for shoulders and place middle 25 (25, 27, 27) back neck sts on holder.

Sleeves

Using smaller needles, cast on 36 (36, 39, 42) sts. Work K2, P1 ribbing for 2½ (2½, 3, 3) in. Incr 1 (1, 0, 1) st in last row of ribbing. Change to larger needles and work next row as follows: K9 (9, 10, 12), P2, K7, P1, K7, P2, K9 (9, 10, 12). Continue to follow chart for chicken-wire pattern for sleeve and also incr 1 st each side every 6th row 6 times. Work until sleeve measures 12 (13, 14, 15) in or desired length to underarm.

Sleeve Cap: Bind off 3 (4, 4, 5) sts beg next 2 rows, dec 1 st each side every knit row until 25 (23, 23, 21) sts remain. Bind off 3 sts beg next 4 rows. Bind off rem 13 (11, 11, 9) sts.

Finishing

Sew left shoulder seam. Using smaller needles, pick up and knit sts on holders and approx 9 (9, 10 11) sts at each neck edge. Work K2, P1 ribbing for 1 inch. Bind off very loosely using a much larger needle. Sew rem seams and weave in ends. Work yellow corn on front using duplicate stitch.

Youth Chicken Pullover

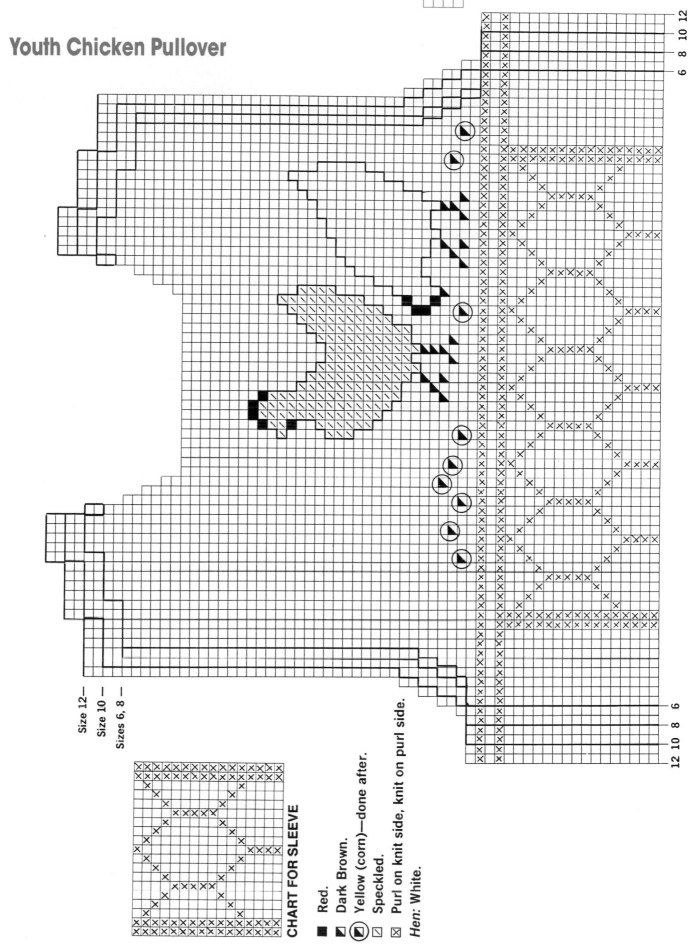

Size 12 —
Size 10 —
Sizes 6, 8 —

CHART FOR SLEEVE

- ■ Red.
- ◤ Dark Brown.
- ⊗ Yellow (corn)—done after.
- ◺ Speckled.
- ⊠ Purl on knit side, knit on purl side.

Hen: White.

Youth Chicken Cardigan

Sizes: 6 (8, 10, 12)
Needles: US 4 and 7—or whatever size
needed to get stitch gauge of 5 sts = 1 in
using Knitting Worsted Yarn.
Materials:
3 (3, 4, 4) 4oz skeins Main Color
10 yds each Pink and Teal for Hens
5 yds Yellow for Legs and Corn
2 yds Plum
Buttons: 6 buttons

Back

Using smaller needles cast on 66 (69, 72,
75) sts. Work K2, P1 ribbing for 2½ (2½, 3,
3) in, incr 1 (2, 3, 4) sts evenly across last
row of ribbing [67 (71, 75, 79) sts]. Change
to larger needles and follow chicken-wire
pattern on chart for back. Work until 10
(11, 11½, 12) in or desired length to
underarm.

Armholes: Bind off 3 (4, 4, 5) sts beg next
2 rows. Dec 1 st each end every knit row 3
(3, 4, 4) times. Work 29 (29, 31, 33) more
rows. Bind off 5 (6, 5, 6) sts beg next 2
rows. Then bind off 5 (5, 6, 6) sts beg next
2 rows. Then bind off 4 (4, 5, 5) sts beg
next 2 rows. Place rem 27 sts on holder.

Directions are for girl's cardigan. Work
buttonholes on left front for boy's cardigan.

Left Front

Using smaller needles cast on 35 (38, 41,
41) sts. Work K2, P1 ribbing on first 30
(33, 36, 36) sts, then seed stitch (K1, P1,
K1, P1, K1) on rem 5 sts.

Next row: K1, P1, K1, P1, K1 first 5 sts,
then K1, P2 across row. Continue in ribbing
to match back; incr 2 (1, 0, 2) sts evenly
across last row ribbing. Change to larger
needles and follow chart for chicken wire
pattern on front.

Armhole: Bind off 3 (3, 4, 5) sts beg next
row. Dec 1 st armhole edge every knit row 3
(3, 4, 4) times. Follow chart until neck.
Work 13 sts at front edge, place on holder,
work across row. Dec 1 st at neck edge every
other row 4 times. Bind off shoulders as per
chart.

Right Front

Work same as left front, only a mirror image,
and work 6 buttonholes evenly spaced on
button band. To work buttonhole: Work to
within 4 sts of end of row, then bind off 2 sts
firmly, finish row. On next row, K1, P1, and
then cast on 2 sts firmly to make buttonhole.
First buttonhole should be halfway up ribbing; last buttonhole should be midway in
neck ribbing, and the other four spaced
evenly between.

Sleeves

Using smaller needles cast on 36 (36, 39,
42) sts. Work K2, P1 ribbing for 2½ (2½, 3,
3) in. Incr 1 (1, 0, 1) st in last row of
ribbing. Change to larger needles and work
next row as follows: K9 (9, 10, 12), P2, K7,
P1, K7, P2, K9 (9, 10, 12). Continue to
follow chart for chicken-wire pattern for
sleeve and incr 1 st each end every 6th row 6
times. Work until sleeve measures 12 (13,
14, 15) in or desired length to underarm.

Sleeve Cap: Bind off 3 (4, 4, 5) sts beg
next 2 rows, then dec 1 st each side every
other row until 25 (23, 23, 21) sts remain.
Bind off 3 sts beg next 4 rows. Bind off rem
13 (11, 11, 9) sts.

Finishing

Sew shoulder seams. Using smaller needles,
pick up and knit sts on holders and approx
9 (9, 10, 11) sts at each neck edge. Work
K2, P1 ribbing for 1 in. Bind off loosely
using a much larger needle. Sew seams and
weave in ends. Sew on buttons.

Youth Chicken Cardigan

- ■ = Plum.
- ◪ = Yellow.
- ⊠ = Purl instead of knit or vice versa.
- ◿ = Teal.
- Hen = Pink.

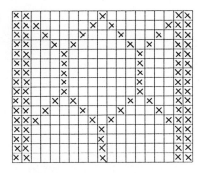

CHART FOR SLEEVE

■ = KNIT ROW

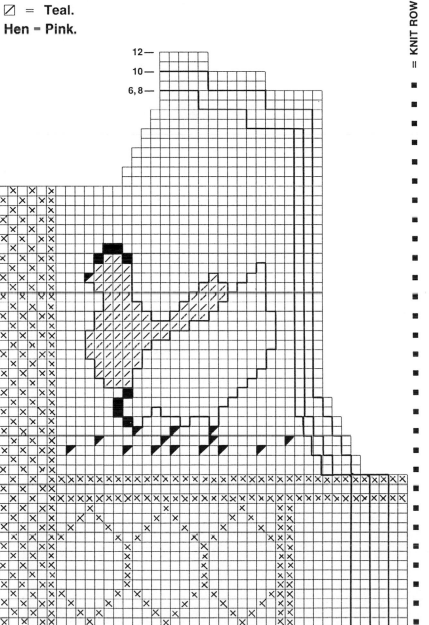

CHART FOR LEFT FRONT

CHART FOR BACK

Teddy Bear Turtleneck

Teddy Bear Turtleneck

Sizes: 6 (8) or 10 (12)

Needles: Sizes 6 and 8—US 4 and 8—or whatever size needed to get stitch gauge of 4½ sts = 1 in. Sizes 10 and 12—US 5 and 9—or whatever size is needed to get stitch gauge of 4 sts = 1 in.

Sweater is worked in Knitting Worsted Weight Wool

Materials:

3 (3, 4, 4) 4oz skcins Main Color

100 yds Center Stripe of Ribbon

100 yds Dark Green

5 yds Medium Brown

2 yds Dark Brown

2 yds Light Brown

Front

Using smaller needles, cast on 61 (66) sts.

Row 1: P1, K1B (knit in back of st), P1, K2. Repeat across row, ending P1.

Row 2: K1, P2, K1, P1, K1, repeat across row, ending K1.

Row 3: P1, K1B, P1, K2 tog, then K first st again before removing from needle to form twist; repeat across row, ending P1.

Row 4: Same as row 2. Repeat these four rows for 2½ in. Incr 5 sts evenly across last row of ribbing [66 (71) sts]. Change to larger needles.

Row 1: K14 (16), work popcorn (K in front, back, front, back, front of the st, then slip 2nd, 3rd, 4th, and 5th st over the 1st to form popcorn), K1, attach bobbin of color A and K1, K1 MC, attach bobbin and K3 Color B, K1 MC, attach another bobbin of Color A and K1, K1 MC, work popcorn, K42 (44).

Row 2 and all even rows: P across row, working colors as indicated.

Row 3: Knit across, working colors as indicated. Repeat these four rows until 7 popcorn rows are completed for size 6; 8 popcorn rows for size 8; 9 popcorn rows for size 10; 10 popcorn rows for size 12. Here's where you decide the length of the sweater. Directions are written for an underarm length of 9, 9¾, 10½, 11¼ in. If you want it longer,

add 4 rows to gain approx ¾ in. Now it is time to start the chart, adding bobbins of color as needed and binding off at armholes when it is time.

Armholes: Bind off 3 sts beg next 2 rows. Dec 1 st each end every knit row 3 times. Continue as per chart until neck.

Neck: Work 20 (22) sts, put rem sts on holder. Dec 1 st neck edge every other row 4 times. Bind off shoulder as indicated on chart. Work other side to correspond.

Back

Work same shaping as front and follow chart for back for placement of colors. Work chart right on up. Place back neck sts on holder.

Sleeves

Using smaller needles, cast on 36 sts. Work ribbing same as front and back for 2½ in. Incr 1 (3) sts evenly across last row of ribbing. Change to larger needles and work 13 (14) sts each side of panel of 11 sts with popcorns and colors [37 (39) sts]. Incr 1 st each end every 6th row 5 (6) times [47 (51) sts]. When ready to work 12th (13th, 14th, 15th) popcorn row, follow chart and dec for armholes as indicated. This will give a finished sleeve-length of approx 11 (12, 13, 14) in.

Sleeve Cap: Bind off 3 (4) sts beg next 2 rows. Dec 1 st each end every knit row until 23 sts remain. Dec 1 st each end every row 4 times. Bind off rem 15 sts.

Neck Ribbing and Finishing

Sew left shoulder seam. Using smaller needle, knit 23 back neck sts, pick up and knit 12 sts along each side of neck plus 15 sts on holder. Work ribbing of K1, P1, for 7 rows. Incr 8 sts evenly across next row. Change to ribbing as for front and back and cuffs, being careful that right side will be showing when neck is turned down. Rib for 2½ in. Bind off loosely using larger needle. Sew seams. Weave in ends.

Teddy Bear—Front

⊞ Color A.   ◪ Color B.

◙ Popcorn.

⊡ Light Brown.   ◺ Medium Brown.

⊠ Dark Brown.

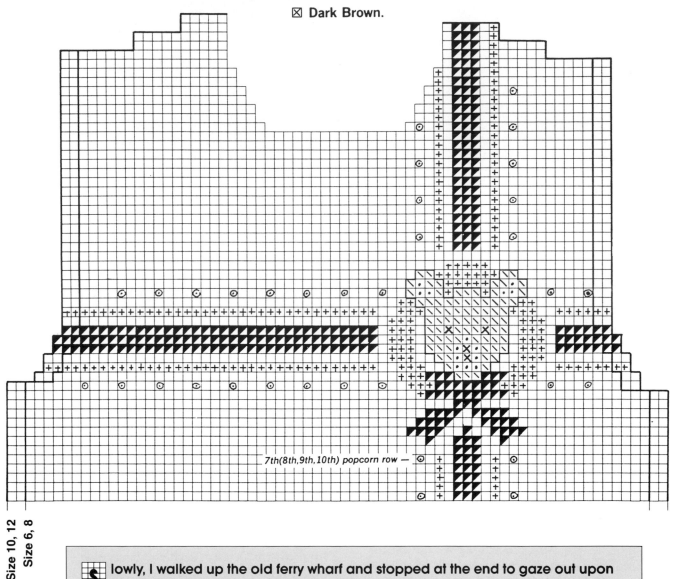

7th(8th,9th,10th) popcorn row —

Size 10, 12

Size 6, 8

Slowly, I walked up the old ferry wharf and stopped at the end to gaze out upon the dark green water that lay flat as glass around the boats and wharves that dot the Thorofare. A light snow fell and hissed as it hit the water creating a fog just over the still water. Then, like a great swan, the ferry rounded the bend and slid into the Thorofare. The top decks were sparsely populated with people, while the bottom deck had several salt-covered cars sitting quietly. When the ferry had made its way into the dock, the captain expertly guided her into the slip with all but a nudge of the piling. Then, with a loud creaking and whining, the ramp was slowly lowered to the deck. Moving to the railing, I watched all the cars as they strained up the steep ramp and crawled to the concrete. Tucking my frozen hands into my cold pockets, I took a last look and then turned and walked quickly off to the store to hang out.

Nathan White, Grade 8

Teddy Bear—Back and Sleeve

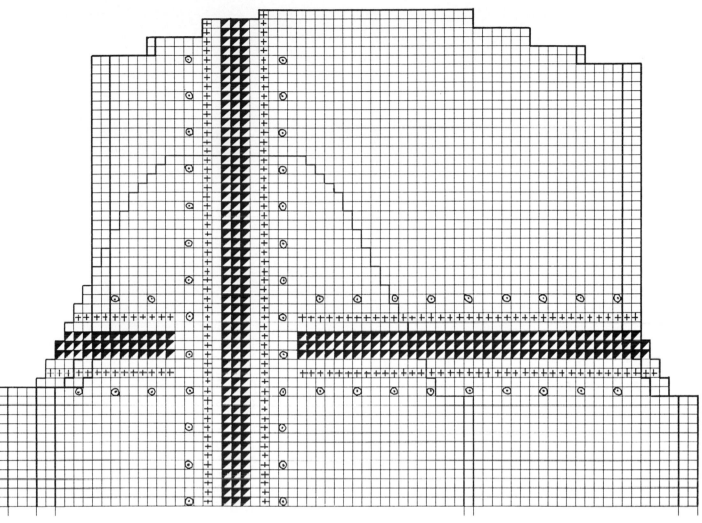

G rowing up on an island is probably really different from growing up anywhere else. The island is usually quiet, even "downtown." The only excitement of going downtown when I was small was going to the candy counter and buying one of each type of candy. I suppose the difference between the island and another place is its friendly ways. Everywhere you walk or drive you always get a friendly "hello" or a smile. When I was young the mailman used to deliver the mail to the box each day. All of the kids would be out at the box awaiting the arrival of the bubble gum he used to through out the window. As children we would wander off all day only to return home for supper. Parents wouldn't fret because the kids were always off building a camp, playing tag or other games. In the city you have to watch your kids. You can't leave them alone for a minute without worrying about them being dragged off or something awful. Even crossing the street was no problem. One car every 20 minutes was all and usually they would slow down if they saw a child anywhere near. Probably the best thing about being a child on the island is you learn to be friendly to everyone, appreciate the small things people do and hope to God you get off before you're a teenager, when everything doesn't seem as **perfect.** *Melanie Cooper, Grade 9*

Tropical Fish Pullover

A Business Within a Business

It's a Thursday and I am at work, concentrating on too many numbers trailing in long columns down the page. The bus stops, the front door opens and several back packs are thrown down in the front hallway. The chaos of many voices and feet pounding up the stairs awakens me to the realization—the kids are working today. Often before they begin their work there is a hurried rush to the store to stock up on snacks. Once returned (if they can pass up the distractions of all of the other kids hanging around the store), the work crew of North Island Bracelets begins their "workday."

I will admit that when my daughter and her friend came up with an idea for their own money making scheme, I was not enthusiastic. Like many other kids they were busy loading up their wrists and ankles with "friendship bracelets" and they could see the possibilities of selling the yarn and directions to other kids in kits. At that time, I was beginning to get a sense of how difficult it was to produce and market a product. I wasn't sure I wanted to get involved with another enterprise where not only would we have to do the same, but I would also have to oversee my daughter and might end up needing to nag her to do the work.

In spite of my concerns, I decided it was a good idea, and went along with the scheme. The two girls were very successful in their first summer—selling the kits through our retail store and even taking the samples around to stores on the mainland looking for a few buyers. Demand was great and one popular store sold over 500 that year before Christmas. The girls were delighted with the money, but it was hard to schedule the work in with all of their other activities. After a little convincing (on my part), the business was turned into a class project with all five students in the then sixth grade class joining in.

They have recently redesigned the letter of introduction that is packed in every kit to state that they are now a class of seventh graders—the class of 1994. The letter also gives a little background about themselves and the smallest school in the state. A set of handwritten directions describes three different styles of bracelets and accompanies eleven colors of yarn in lengths sufficient to make at least three models. Their accounts have grown through word of mouth, an occasional note from us to our retailers about their product, and they now even have a sales representative to whom they pay a commission. They work at least once a week and have generated a good sized savings account from the profits.

Our approach to managing the kids is basically to let them know how many kits have been ordered and then stand back. During the busy periods we pitch in and help a little, but basically the group maintains a moderately constant level of production in spite of the conflicts of basketball teams, a play, after school jobs, and the need to just have fun. It has been

Continued Page 76

Tropical Fish

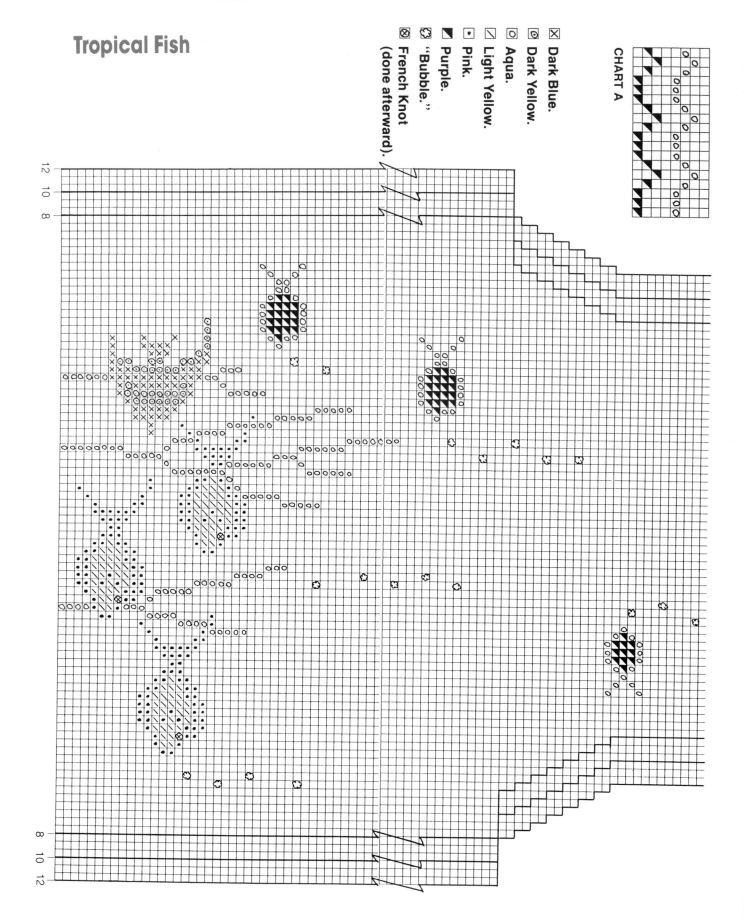

CHART A

⊠ Dark Blue.

⊙ Dark Yellow.

◎ Aqua.

◹ Light Yellow.

▫ Pink.

◤ Purple.

✿ "Bubble."

⊠ French Knot
(done afterward).

Youth Tropical Fish Pullover

Sizes: 8 (10, 12)
Needles: US 4 and 7—or whatever size needed to get stitch gauge of 5 sts = 1 in
Materials:
Sweater is worked in Cotton/Wool Blend
5, (5, 6, 6) 3½oz. skeins Main Color
60 yds Aqua
50 yds Plum
20 yds Bright Pink
20 yds Light Yellow
10 yds Dark Yellow
10 yds Dark Blue

To make "bubbles": K in front, in back, and in front of the same st; turn; P3; turn; K3 tog.

Front

Using smaller needles and Main Color, cast on 68 (74, 80) sts. Work in ribbing as follows:

Rows 1, 3: P1, K2, P1, K1—repeat across row.

Row 2 and all even-numbered rows: P1, K1, P2, K1—repeat across row.

Row 5 and every 6th row thereafter: P1, K2 tog, then reknit first K st to form mock cable, P1, K1—repeat across row.

Continue until ribbing measures 2½ in, incr 10 sts evenly across last row of ribbing. Change to larger needles and work 4 rows stockinette stitch. Work Chart A. Work 0 (2, 4) rows stockinette stitch. Work Main Chart.

(Suggestion: Use bobbins or short strands of color and separate balls of Main Color between "fish" rather than carry colors very far.)

Work armhole when piece measures 11 (12, 13) in or desired length to underarm.

Armholes: Bind of 6 sts beg next 2 rows, then dec 1 st each end every knit row 7 times. [52 (58, 64) sts]. Continue as per Chart until armhole measures 5½ (6, 6½) in.

Neck: Work 16 (19, 22) sts. Bind off center 20 sts. Work rem 16 (19, 22) sts. Working both sides at the same time (attach another ball of yarn), dec 1 st at each neck edge every row 4 (6, 6) times. Place 12 (13, 16) shoulder sts on holders.

Back

Work same as front through Chart A. Parts of Main Chart may be used, or just plain, as desired. You may, for example, wish to do one little fish with bubbles halfway up back. Work armholes same as front until they measure 6 (6½, 7) in. Work across 13 (16, 19) sts, bind off 26 sts, work rem 13 (16, 19) sts. Dec 1 st at neck edge every row 1 (3, 3) times. Place shoulder sts on holder.

Sleeves

Using smaller needles, cast on 38 (38, 40) sts. Work ribbing same as front for 2½ in, incr 6 (7, 8) sts evenly across last row of ribbing. Change to larger needles and work 4 rows stockinette stitch. Work Chart A, and at the same time incr 1 st each end every 6th row 5 (5, 6) times. (Here again, an occasional little fish with bubbles is effective.) Work until sleeve measures 14 (15, 15½) in or desired length to underarm.

Sleeve Cap: Bind off 6 sts beg next 2 rows, then dec 1 st each end every other row until 20 sts rem. Dec 1 st each end every row 4 times. Bind off rem sts.

Finishing

Place shoulders of front and back right-sides together. Using a third needle, knit the shoulders together and bind off the sts. To finish neck, work one row single crochet using a contrasting color. Sew rem seams and weave in ends.

---

ur island is so small that on a map it is not there at all. If you see it from afar, you may think that it is a baseball. *David Boshko, Grade 2*

Child Starry Night Pullover

Child Starry Night Pullover

Sizes: 2 (4, 6)

Needles: US 5 and 8—or whatever size needed to get stitch gauge of 5 sts = 1 in using double strand Sport Weight Wool.

Materials:

700 yds Navy

150 yds Blue

10 yds White

Front

Using smaller needles and Main Color, cast on 60 (64, 68) sts. Work K1, P1 ribbing for 2 in. Change to larger needles and work in stockinette stitch until piece measures 7 (8, 9) in or approx 1 in less than desired length to underarm and then start chart.

Armholes: Bind off 4 (6, 5) sts beg next 2 rows. Dec 1 st each end every knit row 3 times. Work straight as per chart until neck shaping.

Neck: Work 13 (15, 18) sts. Place rem sts on holder. Dec 1 st at neck edge every other row 4 times. Bind off at shoulder edge as per chart. Work other shoulder to correspond, leaving center 16 sts on holder.

Back

Work same as front except neck shaping. Work straight up and bind off shoulders same as front. Place 24 back neck sts on holder.

Sleeves

Using smaller needles, cast on 36 (36, 40) sts and work K1, P1 ribbing for 2 in. Change to larger needles and work in stockinette stitch, incr 1 st each side every 6th row 5 (7, 7) times. [46 (50, 54) sts] Continue until sleeve measures 8 (10, 11) in or approx 1 in less than desired length to underarm and then start chart.

Sleeve Cap: Bind off 3 (5, 5) sts beg next 2 rows. Dec 1 st each end every knit row 7 times, then 1 st each end every row 5 times. Bind off rem sts.

Note:

Block all pieces and embroider stars.

Finishing

Sew left shoulder seam. Using smaller needles and sky color, pick up and knit all available sts around neck including sts on holders. Work in stockinette stitch for 1 in. Next row: *K2 tog, yarn over*, repeat between* across row. Continue in stockinette stitch for 1 in, using larger needle on last row. Bind off very loosely. Turn hem to inside and overcast loosely. Sew rem seams and weave in ends.

The dark frigid waters lapped gently at the weatherworn tar coated pilings that held up the vast wharfs extending from the Brown's Boat Shop. The Fox Island Thorofare looked empty and sullen without all the boats which had hung onto their moorings during the summer months. Heavily, the aromatic smell of freshly planed cedar and wood smoke from the large potbelly stove hung in the warm air of the shop, where a large wooden boat hull sat heavily in the big oak cradles. The pungent odor of fiberglass wafted from a little glass punt being repaired in a far corner. A large barn-style door tugged firmly at the rope that held it tight against the nippy wind blowing outside. *Jerry White, Grade 9*

Child Starry Night—
Front and Back

⊡ = Purl on knit side (or vice versa).
+ = Embroider using White after knitting is completed.

■ = KNIT ROW

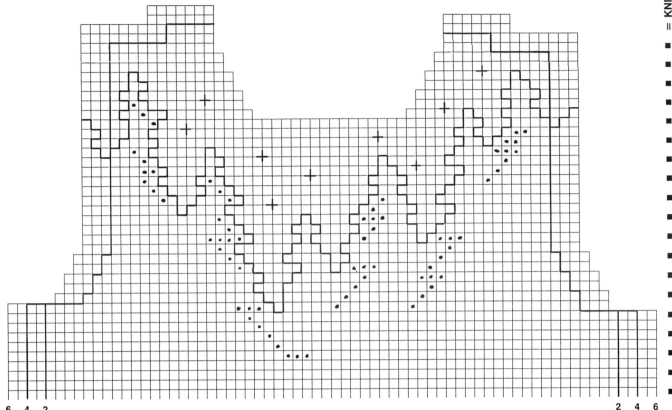

6 4 2   2 4 6

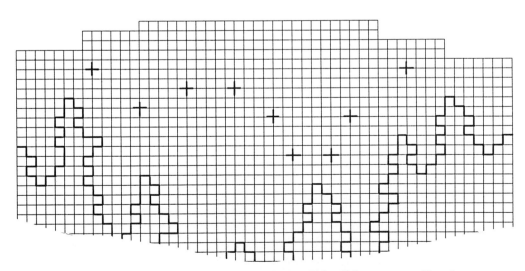

Use this Chart to embroider the Big Dipper on Back.

Child Starry Night— Sleeve Cap

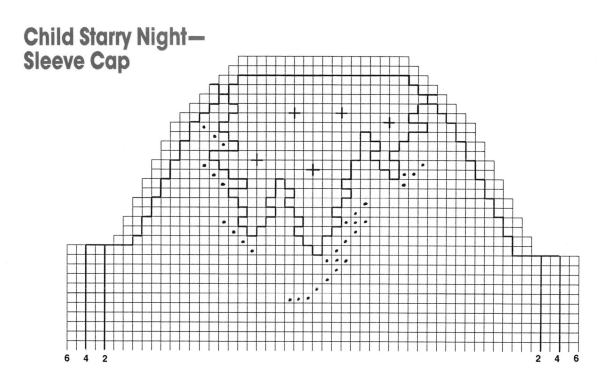

6 4 2   2 4 6

The prettiest place on the island is on the North Shore Road on a small hill at night when the sun is going down over the hills and the twinkling water. This is all I have to say about this pretty place on the island. *Asa Pingree, Grade 2*

In the summer I love to go running. I run on the beaches, on roads, in the woods and on grass. When I run I'm like the wind blowing everywhere, this way and that. When I run a mile or two then I stop and think about where I went so I run home again. When my neighbors' dogs run I run with them anywhere they go. When I get tired I stop and think. I think where I went running the time before this. *Cassie Cooper, Grade 4*

Being a child on North Haven is great. You can do what and go where you want without your parents worrying too much. You don't realize when you are little that there is actually nothing to do. You are content playing on big rocks, going to the beach and riding bikes. But once you are 9 or 10 you begin to get restless and wonder what the rest of the world is like. You are suddenly bored with riding bikes and going to the beach everyday. Once you reach the age of 14 or 15 you are ready to leave the island and feel as though you would never come back. Deep down you know that you'd miss the quiet, peaceful walks, birds singing, fresh air, friendly faces and a feeling of home. *Crystal Beverage, Grade 10*

Night Drive

Driving through our island town at night creates a special feeling. Everything is still, operations ceased until the next day. The ferry, barely illuminated by a few lights, is securely in its slip, a reminder of our islandness. Many houses are dark, their residents gone to bed—sure to be the first ones to greet the next day. Looking in the windows of those that aren't dark reveals a few people milling about or the glow of the TV.

There is a great temptation to look inside each home, with the knowledge that these dwellings are inhabited by people we know and the information garnered will be added to the storage banks of data we collect on each other daily. In a small town this is part of how we maintain our connection with each other—by keeping up on each other's information.

Of course, at times this concern for one another can seem invasive and amount to a feeling of a lack of privacy, but in fact, this is a part of island life and one might as well be resigned to it and see the underlying rewards. In many ways our small town is an extension of the family and the information we collect on each other is not unlike the way family members observe each other. People in small towns who have been there to watch more than one generation have the ability to see individuals as part of a connected family path. We have all been to a family gathering when Aunt Bess observed that our own behavior was not unlike the way her sister had acted during the years they were growing up together—people in small communities make these connections about one another all of the time.

The observations we all make are kept in mind to be pulled out and used the next day or many years later. People often get to know one another so well—each other's habits, routines and working styles—that evoking a name brings about a flood of

associations. Describing an action with one person's name may invoke the vision of a bumbling way to go about something, whereas using another's name invokes a sense of a person with great courage.

On a daily basis, this collection of data is always a reason for conversation—the tie that binds all of us. "I noticed you got all of that wood stacked," or "Were you sick last week? I saw your car at home," become expressions of interest or concern that can prompt a lengthy discussion between those who have little in common in the world of politics or philosophy.

A night drive through town is a time to bring all of those thoughts together. It gives a sense of everything being tucked in—the same secure feeling that comes when checking on the kids. Glancing in a few windows, thinking about our neighbors, having the first look at tomorrow's beginning which, even in the very slow world of a small town, will always bring something new.

Youth Starry Night Pullover

Sizes: 8 (10, 12)
Needles: US 5 and 8—or whatever size needed to get stitch gauge of 5 sts = 1 in using double strand Sport Weight Wool.
Materials:
1200 yds Navy
170 yds Blue
10 yds White

Front

Using smaller needles and Main Color, cast on 70 (74, 78) sts. Work K1, P1 ribbing for 2½ in. Change to larger needles and work in stockinette stitch until piece measures 10 (10½, 11) in or approx 1 in less than desired length to underarm and then start chart.

Armholes: Bind off 5 sts beg next 2 rows. Dec 1 st each end every knit row 3 (4, 4) times. Work straight as per chart until neck shaping.

Neck: Work 18 (20, 22) sts. Place rem sts on holder. Dec 1 st at neck edge every other row 4 times. Bind off shoulders as per chart. Work other shoulder to correspond, leaving center 16 sts on holder.

Back

Work same as front except neck shaping. Work straight up and bind off shoulders same as front. Place 24 (26, 26) back neck sts on holder.

Sleeves

Using smaller needles and MC cast on and work in ribbing same as front, 40 (42, 42) sts. Change to larger needles and work in stockinette stitch, incr 1 st each side every 6th row 7 (8, 8) times. [54 (58, 58) sts]. Continue until sleeve measures 12 (13, 14) inches or approx 1 in less than desired length to underarm and then start chart.

Sleeve Cap: Bind off 5 sts beg next 2 rows. Dec 1 st each end of needle every knit row 10 times. Bind off 3 (4, 4) sts beg next 4 rows. Bind off rem sts.

Note:

Block all pieces and embroider stars.

Finishing

Sew left shoulder seam. Using smaller needles and sky color, pick up and knit all available sts around neck including sts on holders. Work in stockinette stitch for 1 in. Next row: *K2 tog, yarn over,* repeat between * across row.

Continue in stockinette stitch for 1 in. Last row use larger needles. Bind off very loosely. Turn hem to inside and overcast loosely. Sew rem seams and weave in ends.

I live on an island. My grammy and grampy live on another island. We go and visit them sometime. We have to go by a boat. Sometimes it is rough and we get wet. When we get to grammy's house we dry out and have a special time.
Shanna Grant, Grade 3

I like to go exploring through the woods and along the beaches. I like to take pictures and collect interesting things that I find. I have collected arrowheads and a number of feathers. I have recently discovered old stone walls and an old dump that I hope to excavate soon. One of my favorite places to explore is down at the beach not far from my house. I like to stroll down that beach for hours. I find most of my arrowheads down there. I also just like to sit and watch the tide go out when it is getting dark. *Isaiah Parsons, 6th grade*

Youth Starry Night—
Front and Back

☑ = Purl on knit side (or vice versa).
+ = Embroider using White after knitting is completed.

■ = KNIT ROW

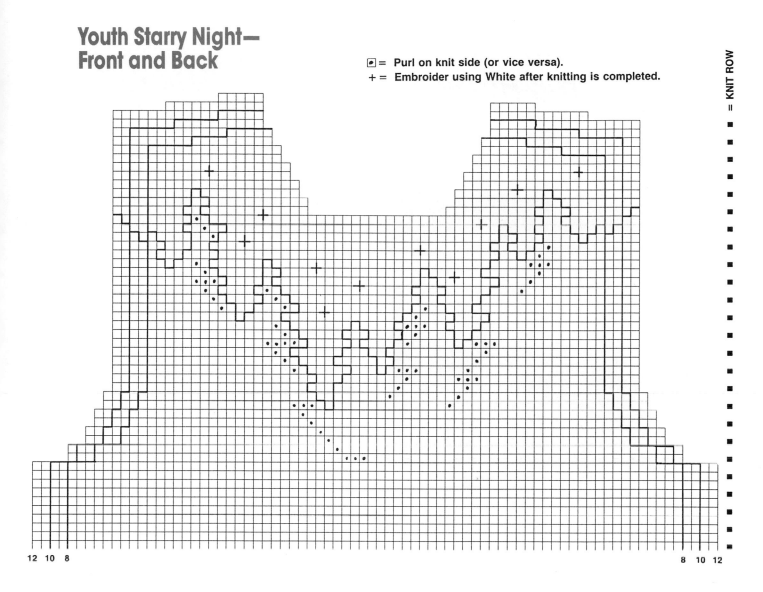

12 10 8   8 10 12

Sleeve Cap

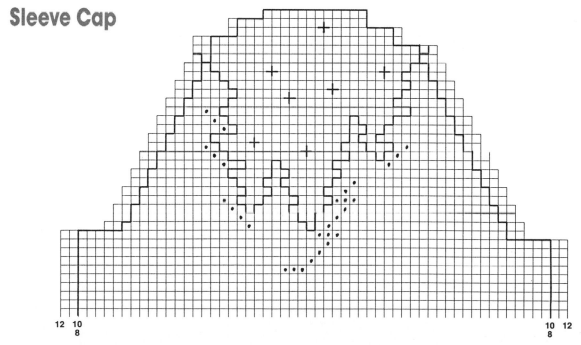

12 10
8   10 12
8

About This Book

Our first book, *Maine Island Classics*, included the history of our business and we thought that describing the production of our knitting books might be a way to continue this story. Producing knitting books seems to have been a natural outgrowth of our company although we still produce sweater kits. The kits allow us to manufacture a "product" which keep us working, the mail plane loaded with UPS packages, and the cash flowing—we hope. All of our new designs begin as kits and our old designs continue to be available in that form as well.

Adding books seemed like a logical way to make all of the knitters who wanted to choose their own yarns happy. So, we began to explore the book business. The standard approach is to find a publisher, submit the materials, wait for the book to appear, and collect the royalties. We had to balance this with another possibility—producing the book ourselves. We could then control the look of the book, choose the photographs, and decide on the format, as well as market the book to the customers we had already accumulated during our years in the kit business. Always looking for a new adventure and having a definite independent streak, this option appealed to us the most—we knew there would be a multitude of decisions to be made and the risks would be far greater, but we jumped in.

The amount of learning that has taken place has been tremendous and the unforeseen pitfalls great, but we are repeating the process in this book, so we must be enjoying the challenge. We work with Michael Mahan and his wonderful team who handle the graphics, design, and production. We continue to learn a great deal from them and have a good time in the process. Working with our photographer, Peter Ralston is fun

and the results make the books enjoyable to look at. Peter has a wonderful way of working with people—making everyone a model and creating stunning photographs from ordinary scenes.

There have been some hard lessons, beginning from day one. We originally had the book put together with a "perfect binding"—the pages glued into the soft cardboard cover. In a fairly short time we realized that the bindings were not "perfect" and that the pages were falling out. By then we had shipped 3,000 copies and we were developing that sinking feeling in the pit of our stomachs. After long negotiations with the printers (our responsibility, since we were the "publishers"), we decided a "recall" was in order and all the books would need to be rebound with a spiral binding.

This of course, was an administrative nightmare and seriously ate into our initial profits. Eventually all the books were rebound and we were pleased to have sold out the first printing of 10,000 within six months. When the second printing began to arrive we could only laugh—the binder had substituted a smaller binding, and the pages fell out as we picked up the first book. At least this time we hadn't shipped any out.

In the broad view this has been a tremendously enriching experience. We have learned a new business, with different marketing channels, another language, and many new opportunities. It has diversified our business and allowed it to grow. It has also given us a chance to put some of our thoughts on paper and share them with you—a process that has been well received and has grown into a regular newsletter, allowing us to stay in touch. To us, this is what the process of being a business is all about—the opportunity to work with other people, be challenged, learn new things, and produce a product that someone will find useful.

A Business Continued

interesting to see how well the kids organize themselves and make rules according to their needs. When they felt that everyone wasn't being conscientious enough, they posted a check-in list and imposed a penalty of 150 extra kits for anyone who missed ten sessions. When they decided that their stops at the store were taking too much time each work day, they took some of their earnings and made a major snack shopping trip so that they could keep after school fuel on hand.

The kids' enterprise is a wonderful way for our business to be involved in a community service project as well as for us to spend some time with the kids. It is difficult to tell whether the friendship bracelet craze will be around to finance them through all of their high school years, but the kids have agreed to work hard for as long as the demand lasts so that if they wake up one day and it is all over they can say—"It was fun while it lasted."

Youth Cable Cardigan Continued

Sleeves

Using smaller needles, cast on 36 (36, 39, 42) sts. Work in K2, P1 ribbing for 2½ (2½, 3, 3) in. Inc 0 (2, 1, 0) sts evenly across last row of ribbing. Change to larger needles and work as follows:

Row 1: K11 (12, 13, 14), P2, K4, P2, K4, P2, K11 (12, 13, 14). Continue working the cables as for front and back, rows 1-11, while incr 1 st each side every 6th row 6 times.

Work until sleeve measures 10 (11, 12, 13) in or 2 in less than desired length of sleeve to underarm. Work cables again (pattern rows 5-11). Work rows 2 and 3 once. Knit next 3 rows to form ridges.

Sleeve Cap: Bind off 2 (3, 3, 5) sts beg next 2 rows. Dec 1 st each end every knit row until 24 (22, 22, 20) sts rem. Bind off 3 sts beg next 4 rows. Bind off rem 12 (10, 10, 8) sts.

Finishing

Sew shoulder seams. Using smaller needles, pick up and knit sts on holders and approx 9 (9, 10, 11) sts at each neck edge. Work in ribbing of K2, P1 for 1 inch. Bind off loosely using a much larger needle. Sew rem seams and weave in ends. Sew on buttons.

he island is small but big enough to live on. The only quiet place in the summer is out on the water hauling traps. The people here are very nice and quiet. They will help you if you are in trouble, got rope in your wheel (boat propeller) or if you're stuck on a ledge. *Jason MacDonald, Grade 8*

About Our Models

In putting together this book we felt privileged to be able to work with so many cooperative and photogenic children and adults. Many are related and we will do our best to sort them out and tell you a little bit about each one.

As you can see we make good use of chickens as well as people. The photo on page 22 is my daughter Cecily, with one of the family hens. These chickens began their stay with the family after Hannah ordered 25 chicks (they come in the mail) and raised them to laying age. They have since passed in ownership through all of the kids as each tired of feeding them and collecting their eggs. Current ownership rests with Cecily who uses most of her egg money at the candy counter. This hen paid Cecily for her good care by leaving a souvenir down the back of the sweater.

The chickens have other ways of getting back at us for our exploitation of them as models. The hen with Kristy, another of our tireless models on page 2, is trying to escape. Kristy is also one of the bracelet kit crew who appear on page 63.

On page 38, Jim MacDonald and his son Jeremiah are shown on the deck of their boat, the Sheila Marie. On page 50 you see Dick Shields and his daughter Jamien. Dick is the captain of our ferry and another of his children, Monica appears on page 63 with the bracelet group. Foy Brown and his nephew Adam appear on page 66 in the family boatyard which recently celebrated its one hundredth year of business.

Cassie and her grandmother Phyllis Cooper appear on page 55, seated on the steps of our store where Phyllis occasionally helps out. She is the mother of 11 and grandmother of 17, no small contribution to a community the size of ours! Page 10 shows grandparents Lewis and Ida Haskell with granddaughter Molly in the Museum. Lewis is one of the island's historians and a collector of memorabilia. He has completely given over 2 rooms off of their home to house his collection. Now the North Island Museum, one room resembles an old fashioned country store and the other has artifacts from farming, fishing and other island occupations. He has also published a book of old stories.

Our other two adult child combinations are not related but photographing them together seemed like a good idea. Eric Hopkins and Siri (Debby's daughter) are shown together in Eric's studio, page 35. Eric is a well known artist who was born here and lives here with his wife Janice and daughter Eva. Janice worked with us until the baby was born last year. My son Asa appears on page 46 with Gil Foltz in the barnyard of Sky Farm. Gil works there as a caretaker—in charge of large houses, healthy sheep and beautiful gardens.

Caleb and Carissa Winslow, brother and sister, appear on pages 14 and 15. They no longer live on the island but are grand-children to the retired postman who always used to have bubble gum for the kids when he delivered the mail (page 61). Michaela Lucey no longer lives here either, but she was visiting her friend Tess on the day we were taking photos. (They appear on page 31.) Tess is a sister to Molly (page 10). Jessie, who was on many of the pages of our last book, is shown with my daughter Hannah on page 58. Hannah looks a few years younger than she does now in the photo of the proprietors of the bracelet kit company. The rest of the kids in the photo are, from left, Katy, Hannah, Kristy, Monica and Nathan.

A pair of twins named Alexander and Jacqueline share a photo with Asa on the back cover. They are regular members of the child care group and alot of fun to play with. On page 75 you will find photos of Debby and me. To tell us apart, remember that I have three children and Debby, although she has five children, (along with two grandchildren) now only has one child at home. Last, there's Stanley (page 74), who delivers our packages and returns with bags of yarn—and often the latest gossip!

Sources of Supplies

In our last book we made one recommendation that we will repeat again. When you are searching out materials, check your local yarn shop and avoid the discount store. The yarn shop owner will most likely be a knowledgeable knitter who can help you with your yarn decisions and will be there when you run into difficult times. Yarn stores are also a dying breed and in need of your support—you'll never know how much you depended on them until they are gone.

However, if you cannot find what you need, all of the materials used in this book are available through us. We sell kits, skeined yarns and yarn packs (all of the yarns used in a pattern without the directions). We also have buttons and wooden knitting needles. You can call us toll free to order or for assistance with one of our patterns. You can also add your name to our mailing list to receive our newsletter—keeping you updated on our designs and stories of island life.

North Island Designs
Main Street
North Haven, Maine 04853
1-800-548-5648
207-867-4788 (Maine and Canada)

For yarn shop owners who would like a list of the sources of supplies used in the book, please contact us and we will be happy to send it to you.

When I awoke and crawled out of bed into the cool crisp air of my room, it was still dark except for a slight glow on the horizon. It looked like it was going to be a wonderful day.

I had no time to lose. I quickly dressed and hurried to the kitchen. I reheated some potatoes; cooked some eggs, bacon and toast; and made some coffee and orange juice. My dad came in from the trap pile where he had been loading the old gray Ford with Lobster traps.

I thought back to the winters when I helped him build many of them. He would skillfully knit the heads and set them with oak laths. He built them all with care because this was the way he made a living.

After I cleaned the breakfast dishes and cleaned up the kitchen, it was time for a day's fishing. I put on an old gray sweat shirt and a pair of dirty sneakers and went out to the truck where Dad was waiting patiently for me. The ride seemed to take forever. I almost thought I was going to burst from the excitement.

As we drove past Kent Cove, the ledges that Goose Rock Light sat on were exposed. The mudflats were also exposed, covered with sandpipers and herring gulls that were trying to get a bit of a snack.

We finally got to the ferry parking lot, which was filled with passengers for the boat. I walked silently through the giant mumbling monster to the ramp that led to the town float. We hopped into the outboard and motored to the "Lucky Lady II."

I was always stuck with two of the worst jobs, banding lobsters or emptying bait bags. Either way, I always did something I hated doing. After a while I got used to it, so I didn't really mind.

I always enjoyed coming back into the harbor just after sunset. Usually there would not be a single ripple on the water except for the wake my dad's boat left behind. It was a great feeling because we were so close to my family's heritage, the sea. *Jessica MacDonald, Grade 12*

n one hot summer day in August, my cousins and I were sitting on the wharf dangling our feet, trying to think of something to do. But, because of the hot weather, we didn't want to do anything real strenuous. Then my cousin said, "I've got it. Let's build a raft and sail around the harbor."

"Yeah, there's tons of old driftwood and logs to build with and then there's some old styrofoam in the brook we could use to help it float," I said excitedly.

So we got up, put our shoes on, and walked up the wharf to my father's and grandfather's shop. The shop is the most interesting place in the world because of all of the tools, paint and many materials for all kinds of projects. The walls are literally covered with old parts to anything that ever moved, wire, tools and ideas for thousands of schemes. In short, a young imaginative boy's dream. Since Nathan, who was about my age, and Lewis, who was about 14, didn't know where anything was in the shop, I was like their jungle guide as we gathered all the necessary tools and supplies.

We went out to the beach and hauled two big logs and a couple of old 2 x 6's to a spot on the beach slightly above the high tide mark. Lewis rolled the logs in place as Nathan and I began to nail the 2 x 6's across the logs. Then we began to nail pieces of old plywood and small lengths of plank to form a platform.

All the while we were working, the tide was rising slowly; so soon we were up to our ankles in water. Then we realized that the raft wouldn't float because it was up too high and the tide wouldn't go up that far.

So I went up and got my outboard and we tied a piece of pot warp to the raft and the other end was tied to my boat. After a while of huffing and puffing from Lewis and Nathan pushing on shore and me out in the boat pulling as much as the little engine could, we finally got the raft in the water. A box in the middle of the raft, a mast, a sheet for sail and a rudder were installed next. Then we were ready to set sail.

I got into my boat again and slowly towed out into the middle of the harbor. We then took the boat in and swam back to the raft. Next, we tried to sail back but our rigging was too crude, so we more or less drifted back to the shore. When we were about 25 to 30 feet from shore, we set our 10 pound mushroom anchor and hoped it would hold. Since it was getting dark, we decided to go home and sleep in my treehouse and try to decide what to do the next day. Thus ended a fun and adventurous day on the water which was the source of so many adventures.

Ryan Haskell, Grade 8

NORTH ISLAND DESIGNS
INCORPORATED

You may contact us directly if you are unable to find any of the materials we have recommended in the book. We have kits, yarn packs (a kit without the pattern) and skeined yarns. We are also here to answer your knitting questions and you can reach us through our toll free number.

If you would like our color brochure or yarn sample cards ($7 ppd) just call or send us one of these postpaid cards. Once your name is on our mailing list, you will receive our quarterly newsletter with descriptions of our latest designs as well as news from the island.

Call our toll free number:
1-800-548-5648
Or in Maine:
1-867-4788
Or send in one of the attached cards.

Please Send Me . . . *Your Catalog and Price List.*

Name_____

Street Address_____

Town_____ State_____ Zip_____

. . . Add a friend to your mailing list!

Name_____

Street Address_____

Town_____ State_____ Zip_____

Phone Orders: 1-800-548-5648 In Maine 1-867-4788

CB

. . . Here are some friends *for your mailing list!*

Name_____

Street Address_____

Town_____ State_____ Zip_____

Name_____

Street Address_____

Town_____ State_____ Zip_____

CB

To Order Books:

Send in the card opposite to order any of our titles.

Since this card goes to a different address, be sure to send in one of the top cards to place your name on *our* mailing list.

To receive a free Down East catalog of fine books and gifts, call **207-594-9544** or **1-800-766-1670**.

Down East Books
P.O. Box 679, Camden, Maine 04843

ORDER FORM

Quantity	Item	Price	Total
	1 — Maine Island Classics	$15.95	
	2 — Maine Island Kids	$15.95	
	3 — Sweaters from the Maine Islands	$16.95	
	4 — North Island Designs 4	$17.95	
		Subtotal	
		Mc. Res. 6% Sales Tax	
		Shipping*	
		TOTAL	

METHOD OF PAYMENT

Mastercard_____ Visa_____ Check_____

Acct. #_____ Exp. Date_____

Signature_____

Name_____

Address_____

_____ Tel._____

*Add $3.25 for first book, $1.00 for each additional book. We ship UPS unless you specify otherwise.

NO POSTAGE
NECESSARY
IF MAILED
IN THE
UNITED STATES

BUSINESS REPLY MAIL
FIRST CLASS   PERMIT NO. 1   NORTH HAVEN, MAINE

POSTAGE WILL BE PAID BY ADDRESSEE

North Island Designs
Main Street
North Haven, ME
04853

NO POSTAGE
NECESSARY
IF MAILED
IN THE
UNITED STATES

BUSINESS REPLY MAIL
FIRST CLASS   PERMIT NO. 1   NORTH HAVEN, MAINE

POSTAGE WILL BE PAID BY ADDRESSEE

North Island Designs
Main Street
North Haven, ME
04853

PLEASE ENCLOSE THIS ORDER FORM
(WITH PAYMENT, IF PAYING BY CHECK)
IN AN ENVELOPE AND
RETURN TO:

Down East Books

P.O. Box 679, Camden, Maine 04843